STUDY IN JEREMIAH

STUDY IN JEREMIAH

by

HOWARD B. RAND, LL.B.

DESTINY PUBLISHERS

Merrimac, Massachusetts 01860

First Edition March, 1947
Second Edition May, 1967

INTRODUCTION

If there were no other reason for writing upon the life and mission of Jeremiah than to refute the oft-repeated statements that this prophet perished in Egypt without completing his divinely appointed commission, it would provide sufficient incentive to retell the life-story of this man of God. Aside from this, however, a knowledge and understanding of the entire scope of Jeremiah's mission—in Palestine, Egypt and in the Isles of the West—rewards the student with a full comprehension of the immensity of the Divine plan concerning God's people today.

There are two primary methods of approach to the study of Scripture. One is the road of scepticism, demanding that evidence and reason precede faith and acceptance. The other is the path of faith, believing God, after which understanding comes. Too often the approach to a study of the life, work and utterances of the prophets is according to the first method, with the result that the truth eludes the search of scholars.

In writing this book it has been our purpose to vindicate the accuracy of the Word of God itself and show that He was not unmindful of the need of keeping all the promises made to Jeremiah, assuring this prophet his life would be preserved to accomplish his full mission. Jeremiah was not only a prophet of doom, predicting destruction for his people, but in fulfilling the final phase of his task, he became a builder and planter. In the last chapter of this book we have shown how this part of his work was carried out in a land far removed from Palestine and Egypt.

Attention is called to the character traits and reactions of a prophet who, though patriotic at heart, had the unpleasant task assigned to him of proclaiming to his people the enormity of their sins, calling upon them to surrender to the enemy. He called for immediate repentance and assured the people that if they failed to heed the call, judgment would certainly follow. When commissioned to preach, Jeremiah was informed that from the very inception of his mission his messages would be unacceptable to the rulers and people alike. However, what cannot be said particularly of any other prophet can be said of Jeremiah, that he lived to witness the full effects of the judgments which he had pronounced upon them and upon the nations of his day. He also lived to lay the foundation of a new and better order in another land and in so doing made a material contribution to the civilization which arose in the west.

This book is written for those who really desire to know the truth about this prophet, his journeys and the place where he was commissioned to build and to plant, for he was called and chosen for this special service even before his birth.

The Author

Merrimac, Mass., 1967

CONTENTS

CHAPTER I

JEREMIAH RECEIVES HIS COMMISSION

There is no sin greater nor so destructive to faith as disbelief in God's commands and promises. In order to secure information from the present day accepted scholars, time has been spent studying Bible dictionaries and reading Bible encyclopedias on Jeremiah without finding a single indication that this prophet, commissioned of God, was able to carry out his full mission. God assigned to him a task to root out, pull down and destroy, and then the most important part of his work, *to build and to plant.* The fulfillment of this final phase of his mission is completely overlooked by the scholars who have written on the life of Jeremiah.

Even when dealing with the written record of the book of Jeremiah, scholars question the authenticity of portions of it and doubt its declared authorship. With such an approach to a study of Jeremiah men are aiding and abetting the multitude of unbelievers in their desire to disprove the Word of God.

JEREMIAH'S MISSION

Because Bible history does not record the fulfillment of this last part of Jeremiah's mission and is silent concerning the prophet's whereabouts, the doctors of divinity, upon arriving at the end of the book and finding no mention of the building and planting, have implied, as well as actually taught, that he failed to complete his mission and died in Egypt. Even the so-called fundamental group follow the lead thus established and also assume Jeremiah died in Egypt early in the 70 year period of Judah's captivity. They, too, are bringing discredit upon the divine origin of this prophet's mission "to build and to plant."

If Jeremiah failed to carry out the latter part of a commission for which he had been called, his authority was not from God, for God never called a man to fulfill a mission without preserving his life for that purpose. If his call was of God, and divinely given, then the work assigned to him must have been completed in its entirety. There is no alternative.

Because Bible students fail to recognize the need of accepting the accuracy of the account of Jeremiah's mission, they have been unable to do other than give an imperfect and far from complete account of this prophet's life. When the facts are made known it will be found that the building and planting phase of his commission is far more important to the nations of the world than the fulfillment of the destructive portion.

BELIEF IN PROPHECY ESSENTIAL

It is the purpose here to present a study of the activities of this prophet of God which will vindicate the record and prove God is true, keeping all His promises and sparing the life of Jeremiah for the completion of his mission. We accept the findings of the scholars that Scriptural history records only the fulfillment of the first phase of Jeremiah's mission: the rooting out, pulling down and destroying. We maintain, however, and can prove that Scripture *prophetically* points to the time and place where the building and planting would occur far removed from the land of Palestine.

Unfortunately, the accuracy of the writings of the prophets mean little or nothing to the scholars and so the clues which should have opened their eyes to the marvelous and more glorious fulfillment of the building and planting phase of Jeremiah's mission are wholly lost to them. Were they willing to accept the inspiration of prophecy there would unfold before them a record of activities in the moves of Israel to the appointed place which would enable them to accurately trace Jeremiah's westward trek. Bible history records the first phase of Jeremiah's mission, prophetically points to the second and secular history records the completion of the building and planting.

JEREMIAH, THE MAN

One characteristic of the book of Jeremiah is that we not only have a fuller account of the life and career of the prophet while in Palestine but we know more about his own inner life and personal feelings than we do of any other prophet. By nature Jeremiah was gentle and tender in his feelings and also sympathetic toward others. Because of his nature God had to make him strong, firm and as unmovable as iron in order to carry out his mission, the first portion of which was to pronounce hard and unmerciful judgment upon his people.

Another marked characteristic of this prophet was his inward spiritual relationship to God.

JEREMIAH'S HOME

Anathoth, the home of Jeremiah, was a city in Benjamin situated about two and a half miles north of Jerusalem. This city was assigned to the priests (I Chron. 6: 60). It was destroyed by the Chaldeans but rebuilt in the time of Nehemiah (Neh. 11: 32). Today nothing remains but a few poor houses on the bleak mountainside, surrounded by mounds of rubbish and hewn stone. Its present condition verifies Jeremiah's denunciation of the city whose young men threatened to kill him if he continued to prophesy in the name of the Lord. History has revealed that cities come under condemnation as well as individuals for their evil acts and Anathoth suffered judgment for the sins of its people.

TIME OF CALL

Contemporary prophets, active during some part of the time when Jeremiah was prophesying, were Daniel, Ezekiel, Habakkuk, Zephaniah and perhaps Obadiah; and it is a Jewish belief that Zechariah was also a contemporary.

Jeremiah was of the priests who were in Anathoth in the land of Benjamin. He was a mere youth when called of God and his commission dates from Josiah's 13th year. This was the year 3377 A.M., or 623 B.C. This young man was called to be a prophet to the nations and the scope of the assigned task is given in the first chapter of his book.

Jeremiah prophesied forty years in Palestine, confining his major work to Jerusalem and this was the final probationary period before Jerusalem was destroyed and the temple burned. The same number of years cover the Acts of the Apostles at the end of which the Temple was again destroyed and the city burned by the Roman Armies.

THE CALL

The detail of Jeremiah's call is set forth in the first chapter of his book where he specifies the times the word of the Lord came unto him. The expression "The word of the Lord came" is a formula almost entirely confined to the two prophets who were priests, Jeremiah and Ezekiel. The account clearly indicates that Jeremiah talked face to face with the Lord and he records the audible speech which passed between them. Just as God spoke to Abraham (Gen. 15: 1-18), and later to Moses, so the Lord God spoke to Jeremiah. In addressing the prophet the Lord said:

"Before I formed thee in the belly I knew thee; and before thou camest forth out of the womb I sanctified thee, and I ordained thee a prophet unto the nations." (Jer. 1: 5.)

Chosen and consecrated for service Jeremiah was selected to be a prophet to the nations before he was conceived in his mother's womb. God in his foresight and foreknowledge knew the type of child who would be born to the parents of Jeremiah whose characteris-

tics when grown to manhood would make him suitable
for His purposes.

GOD GIVES INSPIRATION

Just as Moses tried to excuse himself because of his
speech, so Jeremiah declared he could not speak, his
excuse being that he was but a child, *i.e.*, a young man
perhaps in his early twenties when the call came to him.
One of the interesting facts regarding God's messengers
was their reluctance to accept the responsibilities asked
of them. God selected a type of man in practically every
instance who felt he was neither worthy nor qualified
for the task assigned. Jeremiah was no exception and
when he objected the Lord answered:

"Say not, I am a child: for thou shalt go to all that I
shall send thee, and whatsoever I command thee thou
shalt speak. Be not afraid of their faces: for I am with
thee to deliver thee, saith the Lord." (Jer. 1: 7-8.)

Jeremiah could have refused the call and rejected
the responsibility for all men are created with free-will.
If he had rejected God's demand his personal suffering
would have been great for, as said to Paul, he would
have been kicking against the pricks to his own hurt. But
Jeremiah did not refuse to accept the call. God promised him an audience of those to whom he was to speak.
The Lord then touched Jeremiah's mouth and said:

"Behold I have put my words in thy mouth [made
your mouth eloquent]. See, I have this day set thee over
the nations and over kingdoms, to root out, and to pull

down, and to destroy, and to throw down, to build, and to plant." (Jer. 1: 9-10.)

Isaiah's mouth was touched by the coals from the sacred altar (Isa. 6: 7). Ezekiel was told to open his mouth and not to be rebellious and eat that which was given him. The book which Ezekiel was told to eat contained lamentations, mourning and woe (Ez. 2: 8-10). In every instance the touching of the mouth was a sign of the giving of divine inspiration.

EVIDENCE GIVEN

A double witness of the certainty of Jeremiah's call and of coming judgment was next given. First the prophet saw a rod of an almond tree. Ferrar Fenton translates this, "I see the branch of a watchful tree!" Now the almond tree signifies a watcher or early waker because it is the first of the trees to wake from its winter sleep. The almond tree stands in its relation to the trees as the cock stands in his relation to the birds. A rod or staff is for striking. The Lord informed Jeremiah that he was to attend to what he saw for He is watchful over His promises to perform them.

The Lord asked Jeremiah the second time what he saw and Jeremiah said:

"I see a seething pot; and the face thereof is toward the north." (Jer. 1: 13.)

In order to complete the message and indicate that it was the fulfillment of the words of judgment, a boiling cauldron was shown on which fire was being blown, or fanned, from the north. From the north evil was to come and the enemy [Babylon], though situated in the east, would come around the desert and advance against Jerusalem from the north, the usual route from Assyria. This would bring evil and calamity upon Jeremiah's people for the Lord said:

"Lo, I will call all the families of the kingdoms of the north, saith the Lord; and they shall come, and they shall set every one his throne at the entering of the gates of Jerusalem, and against all the walls thereof round about, and against all the cities of Judah. And I will utter by judgments against them touching all their wickedness, who have forsaken me, and have burned incense unto other gods, and worshipped the works of their own hands." (Jer. 1: 15-16.)

DOUBLE WITNESS IMPORTANT

The question of witnessing is important for God requires man to weigh evidence and accept testimony in conformity with the requirements for establishing facts. The giving and weighing of evidence not only applies in matters affecting man's relationships with man but it also governs God's dealings with men. God does not ask us to accept facts without evidence to sustain them. His dealings with us are based upon testimony which conforms with the requirements of the law:

"One witness shall not rise up against a man for any iniquity or for any sin, in any sin that he sinneth: At the mouth of two witnesses, or at the mouth of three witnesses, shall the matter be established." (Deut. 19: 15.)

When, however, God has given full and adequate

proof of a matter, in conformity with this law of juris-
prudence, He rightly expects men to accept the facts to
which the evidence testifies. Failure to do so brings
condemnation.

Moses was called of God to lead the Israel people
from Egypt, but he demurred. The Lord dealt patiently
with him until the double witness had been given in
turning Moses' rod into a serpent and making his hand
white with leprosy. When Moses still continued his
objections in face of this evidence, God was angry with
him.

Later God called Gideon to lead Israel against the
Midianites. Gideon asked a test of the Lord and was not
satisfied until a double witness was given. Accepting
this evidence he went forth and led Israel to victory. In
the days of Joseph, Pharaoh dreamed a dream which
was doubled to him because, according to Joseph, "the
thing is established by God."

Nebuchadnezzar dreamed a dream but not until it
was doubled, in that Daniel also had the vision, was it
made certain and the interpretation thereof sure.

There was no place for repentance for Sodom and
Gomorrah yet Nineveh could repent. Why? The answer
is found in the fact that two witnesses appeared against
the cities of the plain when two Angels entered the
streets of Sodom and the doom of these cities was sealed.
In the case of Nineveh one prophet only was sent to
testify against her and that city repented and was saved
for the time being. Many more such instances in Scripture could be cited but the above sufficiently establishes

the certainty of a thing for which a double witness is given.

Jeremiah was given a double witness in the vision of the almond tree and the boiling cauldron. Ever afterward Jeremiah testified to the certainty that Babylon would destroy the city and temple. This colored his thought and gave him assurance of his testimony and a positive stand against the evils being committed by his people. True, the disaster was long in coming but Jeremiah could afford to wait even though at times, during his forty years of witnessing and prophesying, he was labeled a fanatic and false prophet.

GOD STRENGTHENS JEREMIAH

Having given Jeremiah evidence of the certainty of judgment to come and of the fulfillment of his promises God prepared to strengthen the prophet for the task which lay before him.

"Thou therefore gird up thy loins, and arise, and speak unto them all that I command thee: be not dismayed at their faces, lest I confound thee before them."

The prophet is thus to prepare for trouble as he makes ready to meet strong opposition but God declares:

"Behold, I. have made thee this day a defensed city, and an iron pillar, and brasen walls against the whole land, against the kings of Judah, against the princes thereof, against the priests thereof, and against the people of the land. And they shall fight against thee: but they shall not prevail against thee; for I am with thee, saith the Lord, to deliver thee." (Jer. 1: 18-19.)

PROMISE OF PROTECTION

What a mission to give to a young man! The civil authorities would oppose him, the nobility would fight against him, the ecclesiastical leaders would seek to destroy him and the people would be excited against him. God did not promise Jeremiah any support from human sources in carrying out his mission. God did, however, promise that though every man would be against him they would not prevail for God would deliver him from all his enemies. Jeremiah was given assurance that we was to be as a strong city of defense against every attack.

The closing verses of the first chapter amount to an explicit guarantee of personal immunity from all serious bodily harm to Jeremiah himself. In view of this promised protection it is manifest that all the legends which have attributed his disappearance to eventual martyrdom, current among Jews and Christians alike, are utterly baseless. It is a choice between accepting the promises made by God or disbelief. There should be no hesitation as to which side the man of faith will take. Jeremiah suffered much at the hands of his enemies, yet God delivered him from their power as he declared the message God had laid upon him and *lived* to build and plant in another land far removed from Palestine. As a prophet to the nations he carried out the full requirements of his office and completed his entire mission.

CHAPTER II

THE PROCLAMATION TO JUDAH AND ISRAEL

Immediately following the receipt of his commission Jeremiah, then residing in Anathoth, was called to go to Jerusalem. He continued to retain his connection with Anathoth though his mission to root out, pull down and destroy was to be announced in the city of David. Following God's instructions, he went to Jerusalem to proclaim his first message:

"Go and cry in the ears of Jerusalem, saying, Thus saith the Lord." (Jer. 2:2.)

The prophet, becoming Jehovah's oracle, addressed the nation and condemned the House of Judah for their sins. As God's mouthpiece the prophet reminded Judah how they had been attended in their infancy, loved and guided through the wilderness and brought into Palestine. The prophet then increased the scope of his message to include the House of Israel:

"Hear ye the word of the Lord, O house of Jacob and all the families of the house of Israel." (Jer. 2:4.)

JEREMIAH CONDEMNS EVIL

Speaking in the name of the Lord, the prophet asked what injustice had their fathers found in the Lord that they should turn from Him and why were they deluded into following after vain things and idols? Why had they become vain, for idolaters always become like the gods they worship.

Jeremiah reminded them that they had not asked where the Lord was who brought them out of Egypt and led them through the wilderness. He informed the people that God had brought them into a plentiful country to eat its fruit and enjoy its goodness but they had defiled His land with the worship of abominable things.

Even the priests did not ask for the Lord or teach His laws, nor did the pastors instruct the people regarding Him. Instead they taught about Baal and refused to follow their own God. Because of these evils Jeremiah declared God will contend with them, even with their sons and their son's sons. The nation is accused of turning from the living God to accept heathen gods, which are no gods at all:

"My people have committed two evils; they have forsaken me, the fountain of living waters, and hewed them out cisterns, broken cisterns, that can hold no water." (Jer. 2: 13.)

This people, having turned to idolatry and forsaken the Lord, is likened by the prophet to wells without water when they might have possessed the fountain of Living Water. The question is asked if Israel is a slave and why they have become spoiled. The answer is given by Jeremiah who declares these conditions have come upon his people because they forsook the Lord their God who had led them in the past. He calls upon them to turn from their evil ways and learn how bad

and rebelliously forgetful they were of the Lord their
God. Though in the past the people had declared they
would not do such evil things, or transgress the commands of their living God, yet they did wander away,
playing the harlot and serving idols. God had planted
them a noble vine unto Him but their evil became
so great Jeremiah declared:

"For though thou wash thee with nitre [a mineral
alkali used in Palestine as a compound for soap], and
take thee much soap, yet thine iniquity is
marked [engraven] before me, saith the Lord God."
(Jer. 2: 22.)

THE PEOPLE ANSWER

It is evident from the context that the people answered the prophet by declaring they had not gone after
Baal and so Jeremiah replied:

"How canst thou say, I am not polluted, I have not
gone after Baalim [false gods generally including
Moloch]?" (Jer. 2: 23.)

Specific cases of transgression are pointed out and
though the people thought their doings were hidden
from Jeremiah the prophet declared he knew of their
proceedings in the valley where they worshipped idols,
and of their feasts of lust and depravity. He then declared them like a wild ass, accustomed to the desert,
who in the spirit of lust love wantonness. Addressing
the House of Israel Jeremiah declared of them:

"As the thief is ashamed when he is found, so is the
house of Israel ashamed; they, their kings, their princes,

and their priests, and their prophets, saying to a stock [wood or tree in idolatrous worship], Thou art my father; and to a stone, Thou hast brought me forth [possible allusion to the Stone of Israel which went with them through the wilderness and which had become an object of idolatrous worship]: for they have turned their back unto me, and not their face: but in the time of their trouble they will say, Arise and save us." (Jer. 2:26-27.)

Jeremiah chided them, asking the whereabouts of the gods which they had made? Let them arise and save the people in a time of trouble for they had set up as many gods as there were cities in Judah. Speaking for the Lord, Jeremiah declared:

"Wherefore will ye plead with me? ye all have transgressed against me, saith the Lord." (Jer. 2:29.)

God declares that though He pleaded with them and corrected their children they have killed His prophets like a destroying lion. The question is asked:

"Can a maid forget her ornaments, or a bride her attire? Yet my people have forgotten me days without number." (Jer. 2:32.)

Judah is accused of having the blood of the innocent upon her garments and God will plead with them because she says, "I have not sinned."

THE DIVORCED WOMAN

Jeremiah reminded Judah of the keen disappointment they suffered when looking to the Egyptians and to the Assyrians for help for God had rejected those nations in whom they had trusted. The prophet then cites the case of a divorced woman and asked:

"If a man put away his wife, and she go from him, and become another man's, shall he return unto her again? shall not that land be greatly polluted?" (Jer. 3: 1.)

Under the law a man was forbidden to take again to wife a woman whom he had divorced if she had become the wife of another, even though her second husband should die. The law states:

"Her former husband, which sent her away, may not take her again to be his wife, after that she is defiled; for that is abomination before the Lord: and thou shalt not cause the land to sin, which the Lord thy God giveth thee for an inheritance." (Deut. 24: 4.)

The prophet continues in his condemnation of Judah for her idolatry and for having played the harlot with many lovers yet undertaking to again return to the Lord. It is because of these evils that rain was withheld from the land as the people went their own way and walked contrary to the laws of God.

A MESSAGE TO ISRAEL

God asked Jeremiah in the days of Josiah:

"Hast thou seen that which backsliding Israel hath done? she is gone up upon every high mountain and under every green tree, and there hath played the harlot." (Jer. 3: 6.)

This refers to the northern ten tribed Kingdom who had turned away from God to follow after idolatry.

They had set up their idols on the hills and in the groves where heathen rituals were carried on. The Lord calls her to return to him and though she returned not the expression "Turn thou unto me" implies in its Hebrew meaning *"Unto me she will return"* and is prophetic of a future turning of the House of Israel to God. Judah had seen what had happened to Israel, God allowing her enemies to overcome Samaria and carry the people away into captivity, for the northern Kingdom was deported and taken to Assyria. The fact of Israel's divorcement is set forth by the prophet:

"And I saw, when for all the causes whereby backsliding Israel committed adultery I had put her away, and given her a bill of divorce; yet her treacherous sister Judah feared not, but went and played the harlot also." (Jer. 3: 8.)

God in no particular ever confuses the House of Israel with Judah. This passage clearly indicates they are two separate and distinct peoples, for Israel was divorced while Judah was not. The significance of the divorcement of one and not of the other is completely lost to those who have failed to recognize the distinction between the two.

As has already been stated, under the law when a woman was divorced she not only ceased to be the wife of the one writing the bill of divorcement but if she married another, though her second husband died, she could not again become the wife of her first husband. When God gave Israel a bill of divorcement Israel ceased to be His people. Under the law they could not return to Him again for they had followed after Baalim.

JUDAH COMMITTED ADULTERY

Judah knew all this and yet feared not to feign to be true to God while playing the harlot by committing adultery with stones and with stocks (the material out of which idols were made). * The reformation under Josiah was instigated by the King alone for the people's hearts were not changed. The Lord said to Jeremiah that backsliding Israel had justified herself more than treacherous Judah and so the prophet is told to proclaim these words toward the north as a message to the House of Israel who had been taken into Assyrian captivity.

A CALL TO ISRAEL

"Return, thou backsliding Israel, saith the Lord; and I will not cause mine anger to fall upon you: for I am merciful, saith the Lord, and I will not keep anger forever. Only acknowledge thine iniquity, that thou hast transgressed against the Lord thy God, and haste scattered thy ways to the strangers under every green tree and ye have not obeyed my voice, saith the Lord." (Jer. 3: 12-13.)

THE WAY PROVIDED

But how could Israel return to God who had given her a bill of divorcement and put her away? Under the law she was forever barred from being His people again.

* See "Provoking the Wrath of God, DESTINY for August, 1945.

The additional testimony of Hosea, the Prophet, is valuable in the discussion of this important subject for his entire book is devoted to a demonstration of the position of the Lord God of Israel as the husband of His People. Hosea graphically illustrates Israel's condition in the naming of his two sons, Jezreel and Lo-Ammi. In Jezreel he depicts Israel's falling away from God and in naming his second son Lo-Ammi, their divorced state. He then looks forward to the day when Israel will again become God's people but under the terms of the New Covenant. Now Lo-Ammi means "not my people" for God told the prophet that in thus naming his son His message to Israel was,

"Ye are not my people, and I will not be your God." (Hosea 1: 9.)

Immediately following this is the promise of a multitudinous growth of the Israel people at some future time:

"Yet the number of the children of Israel shall be as the sand of the sea, which cannot be measured nor numbered; and it shall come to pass, that in the place where it was said unto them, Ye are not my people, there it shall be said unto them, Ye are the sons of the living God." (Hosea 1: 10.)

This is a remarkable prophecy of the future greatness of Israel for, after Hosea had declared Israel would not be His people, the prophet points to the expansion and growth of the House of Israel whose identity would be lost to themselves and unrecognized by the nations around them. Yet, with it all, a mark of identification in the latter days was to be their own declaration that they are the sons of the living God and thus a Christian people.

Hosea points to the hopeless condition of Israel due to her divorced state and the hardships she must endure, climaxing his statements with the hope and promise of a time to come when the Lord will fulfill:

"I will sow her unto me in the earth; and I will have mercy upon her that had not obtained mercy; and I will say to them which were not my people, Thou art my people; and they shall say, Thou art my God." (Hosea 2: 23.)

THE PROMISE OF DELIVERANCE

In no way does Hosea explain the process by which the bill of divorcement under which Israel was put away is annulled. How was Israel to be set free from the curse of the law that she might again become God's people? The answer is given by Isaiah in a message addressed to the daughters of Israel:

"Where is the bill of your mother's divorcement, whom I have put away? or which of my creditors is it to whom I have sold you? Behold, for your iniquities have ye sold yourselves, and for your transgressions is your mother put away." (Isa. 50: 1.)

God is not asking these questions for information but rather in the sense of affirming the fact that Israel had been divorced. He states His case against Israel, giving the reasons why she was put away. Recognizing that

Israel knew the apparent hopelessness of her position under the law of divorcement, God declares:

"Is my hand shortened at all, that it cannot redeem? or have I no power to deliver?" (Isa. 50: 2.)

Having asked this question, God issues a call to His people Israel:

"Hearken to me, ye that follow after righteousness, ye that seek the Lord: look unto the rock whence ye are hewn, and to the hole of the pit whence ye are digged." (Isa. 51: 1.)

This message is directed to the same people who, according to Hosea, have been declaring they are not God's people. They are now called to recognize their identity:

"Look unto Abraham your father, and unto Sarah that bare you." (Isa. 51: 2.)

Such a message would only be addressed to a people who had lost the knowledge of their origin. As God proceeds to address this people he exclaims:

"Awake, awake; put on thy strength, O Zion ... For thus saith the Lord, Ye have sold yourselves for nought, and ye shall be redeemed without money." (Isa. 52: 1-3.)

ISRAEL TO BE REDEEMED

Then follows the promise of redemption so clearly set forth in the fifty-third chapter of Isaiah. The redemption is accomplished through the death of the Son of God (the Lord God of the Old Testament), the husband who had divorced Israel. Though Israel was set free from the curse of the law, further provision had to be made by which she could again be recovenanted to God.

THE TESTATOR

Jesus Christ was not only the redeemer of Israel but He also was the Testator of a new covenant which, having the nature of a will, would not be in force until after His death. The writer of Hebrews clearly sets forth this fact:

"For where a testament is, there must also of necessity be the death of the testator. For a testament is of force after men are dead: otherwise it is of no strength at all while the testator liveth." (Heb. 9: 16-17.)

This is true of any "will" made by man for not until his death will his "will" become valid. The same was true of the New Covenant of which Jesus Christ was the Testator. When our Lord Jesus Christ came and died that Israel might be redeemed He wrought salvation for every individual and sealed the terms of the New Covenant in His blood.

The redemption of Israel did not include Judah because the House of Judah was not divorced, nor did she lose her identity as a portion of God's people. To redeem means to regain possession of that which was once owned and lost. Israel, being divorced, was in need of redemption in order to be restored to her Lord. Judah, being judged for sin and idolatry, was in need of a Saviour. Both would find in Jesus Christ, Redeemer and Saviour, the way opened to be recovenanted to God under the "will", or testament, of Jesus Christ, the Testator.

GOD'S PROMISE TO ISRAEL

Anticipating His work of redemption, God through Jeremiah continues His message to Israel:

"Turn, O backsliding children, saith the Lord; for I am married unto you: and I will take you one of a city, and two of a family, and I will bring you to Zion." (Jer. 3: 14.)

When Israel returns the Lord promises that He will give them pastors who will instruct them with knowledge and skill. They are informed that the Ark of the Covenant shall not be remembered, nor will they grieve about it for the Throne of the Lord will be at Jerusalem. In that day all nations will acknowledge the Lord and there shall be no more perversion or suffering.

Israel and Judah are to walk together at that time for both will be of the same spirit. God even declares Israel will then possess a pleasant land and splendid armies. Addressing Israel, the Lord proclaims:

"Thou shalt call me, My Father; and shalt not turn away from me." (Jer. 3: 19.)

This prophecy is being fulfilled today in the Anglo-Saxon-Celtic peoples who possess a pleasant land and splendid armies and as Christians call God their father. Anticipating the coming of this day, God through Jeremiah calls to Israel:

"Return, ye backsliding children, and I will heal your

backslidings [or restore us from our wanderings]."
(Jer. 3:22.)

ISRAEL'S RESPONSE

Following God's call to His people Jeremiah prophetically records the response to that call:

"Behold, we came unto thee: for thou art the Lord
our God. Truly in vain is salvation hoped for from the
hills, and from the multitude of mountains: truly in
the Lord our God is the salvation of Israel. For shame
hath devoured the labour of our fathers from our
youth; their flocks and their herds, their sons and their
daughters. We lie down in our shame, and our confusion covereth us: for we have sinned against the Lord
our God, we and our fathers, from our youth even unto
this day, and have not obeyed the voice of the Lord our
God." (Jer. 3:22-25.)

GOD ANSWERS THE PEOPLE

"If thou wilt return, O Israel, saith the Lord, return
unto me: and if thou wilt put away thine abominations
out of my sight, then shalt thou not remove. And thou
shalt swear, The Lord liveth, in truth, in judgment, and
in righteousness; and the nations shall bless themselves
in him, and in him shall they glory." (Jer. 4: 1-2.)

When His people heed this call and turn to God
there will be fulfilled in its completeness the promise
made to Abraham, "In thee shall all families of the
earth be blessed."

CHAPTER III

GOD'S CONTROVERSY WITH JUDAH

After Jeremiah had delivered a message to the House of Israel calling upon them to return to the Lord, prophetically declaring the day of that return, the prophet turned his attention to Judah and Jerusalem. Addressing them as he continued his message in the fourth chapter of his book, he summoned the inhabitants of the city to circumcise their hearts lest God's fury be poured out upon them for their evil doings.

This is one of three passages in the Old Testament referring to spiritual, or Christian, circumcision. The first reference is in Deut. 10: 16 wherein Moses, after declaring God's requirements that Israel fear Him, love Him, serve Him and keep His commandments, called upon the people to circumcise their hearts and become spiritually in tune with Him. The second mention of this type of circumcision is in Deut. 30: 6 when Moses prophetically declares the day will come when God will circumcise their hearts and the hearts of their seed, to love the Lord their God with all their hearts and with all their souls that they may live. Though this same type of call is issued to the inhabitants of Jerusalem by Jeremiah, the prophet anticipates their refusal and foretells war for Judah:

"Declare ye in Judah, and publish in Jerusalem; and say, Blow ye the trumpet in the land . . . I will bring evil from the north and a great destruction." (Jer. 4: 5-6.)

Babylon did not lie toward the north but was east of Judea. No army, however, could keep itself in supplies in a march directly eastward through the desert of Arabia. The Babylonians would, according to custom and convenience, cross the Euphrates and enter Judea from the north through Syria and Damascus. Jeremiah, knowing this, referred to Babylon in the following terms:

"The lion is come up from his thicket, and the destroyer of the Gentiles is on his way; he is gone forth from his place to make thy land desolate; and thy cities shall be laid waste without inhabitant." Jer. 4: 7.)

REASON FOR COMING CAPTIVITY

Thus the captivity of Judah is foretold when all the inhabitants would be carried away to Babylon. The reason given is:

"Because she hath been rebellious against me, saith the Lord. Thy way and thy doings have procured these things unto thee; this is thy wickedness, because it is bitter, because it reaches unto thine heart." (Jer. 4: 17-18.)

Previously Jeremiah had pointed out that in the day Judah went into captivity courage would perish from the hearts of the rulers and this led him to exclaim:

"Ah Lord God! surely thou hast greatly deceived this people and Jerusalem saying, Ye shall have peace; whereas the sword reaches unto the soul." (Jer. 4: 10.)

The expression "greatly deceived" is the translation of an Hebrew idiom declaring that they would be deceived. While God had promised peace to a penitent people who would forsake their idolatry and return to the Lord, the people of Judea appropriated the promise without complying with the conditions and, in listening to the false prophets who prophesied peace, they were deceived.

The fact that the sins of Judah were of the heart, deliberate and planned, indicated they had reached a condition wherein they had no desire to repent. They wished only to escape punishment for their evil doings. Jeremiah recognized this and lamented over the prospects of the trouble that he knew was inevitable. He exclaims:

"I am pained at my very heart . . . I cannot hold my peace, because thou hast heard, O my soul, the sound of the trumpet, the alarm of war." (Jer. 4: 19.)

THE LAND TO BE DESOLATE

Visualizing the coming calamities which were to afflict his native land, Jeremiah speaks of destruction upon destruction, with the whole land spoiled, and then declares of his people:

"They have none understanding: they are wise to do evil, but to do good they have no knowledge." (Jer. 4: 22.)

Because of the severity of the coming disaster, which would empty the land of its inhabitants, the prophet is reminded of a former great catastrophe, when the earth became void and without form, which he uses as an illustration of the completeness of the destruction about to overtake his native land. Past, present and future are within the vision of the prophetic eye and thus Jeremiah is inspired to recount the conditions which were extant in the world after the great destroying judgment which left the earth in the condition described in the second verse of the first chapter of Genesis, the cause of which he declares was the sins of a pre-Adamic race:

"I beheld the earth, and, lo, it was without form, and void; and the heavens, and they had no light. I beheld the mountains, and, lo, they trembled, and all the hills moved lightly. I beheld, and, lo, there was no man, and all the birds of the heaven were fled. I beheld, and, lo, the fruitful place was a wilderness, and all the cities thereof were broken down at the presence of the Lord, and by his fierce anger." (Jer. 4: 23-26.)

This overwhelming destruction upon a pre-Adamic age was used by Jeremiah in an attempt to drive home to the people of Judah and Jerusalem the overwhelming nature of the disaster about to engulf them. Addressing the people, the prophet informed them that their land was to become desolate and the whole city would flee before the invading armies, with the people trying to hide in the thickets and among the rocks.

Jeremiah addressed Judah as though he were talking to an eastern harlot who had decked herself in fine clothes, thinking to curry the continuing favor of her lovers by her fairness. Actually, Jeremiah pointed out, they will become her spoilers. Because of the inevitability of coming disaster Judah's anguish is to be like that of the inescapable trouble of a woman in travail.

AN EXTRAORDINARY BARGAIN

God challenges Jeremiah to see if he can find an honest man in Jerusalem—one who executes judgment and seeks truth. If so, he will pardon the city.

"Run ye to and fro through the streets of Jerusalem, and see now, and know, and seek in the broad places thereof, if ye can find a man, if there be any that executeth judgment, that seeketh the truth; and I will pardon it." (Jer. 5: 1.)

A similar issue was raised when Abraham requested the Lord to spare Sodom and Gomorrah from destruction. He limited the final count to ten righteous men who, if found in those cities, would save them from destruction. God is willing to pardon Jerusalem if Jeremiah can find but one righteous man in the city. Failing to do so, the city would be adjudged completely unrighteous.

The result of Jeremiah's search revealed that the poor retained only a form of religion but had forsaken the Lord, while the rich had become avowed infidels and libertines. The failure to produce one man in the entire city who was righteous brought confirmation of the judgment upon Judea, Jerusalem, its rulers and the people, for God declared it impossible to pardon such offenses as were being committed.

JUDGMENT CONFIRMED

Punishment being no longer delayed, the prophet was

commanded to remove Judah's defenses as God declared
that both the Houses of Israel and Judah were under
condemnation, neither having been true to Him. The
leaders and the people were saying God is nothing (the
speech of the atheist), nor would they believe the predicted troubles of sword and famine would ever overtake them. The false prophets and preachers came under
condemnation for they were not guided by the Spirit of
the Lord but preached messages out of their own hearts
to gain popular favor, which Jeremiah labeled falsehoods. And so the prophet declared:

"Because ye have abandoned Him and served foreign
gods in your own country,—therefore you shall serve
tyrants in a country not your own." (Jer. 5: 19, *F. F.
Trans.*)

This judgment was to be communicated to the House
of Israel and reported throughout all Judea, for the
people are declared to be foolish and without understanding hearts or else they would have turned to God,
the one who had given them their past prosperity and
blessed their harvests. The prophet proceeded to point
out that wicked and treacherous men, leaders in the
nation, had enriched themselves at the expense of their
fellow men. They were fat and rich and dealt in false
evidence, regarding neither the rights of the widow nor
the orphan. God declared that if the heathen did such
things He would avenge the wrongs and then asks,
should He not punish His people for these evils?

RELIGIOUS LEADERS CONDEMNED

Turning his attention to the ecclesiastical leaders, Jeremiah denounced them for preaching lies and practicing deceit. The situation was further complicated by the fact that the people loved to have it so. The prophet declared there is nothing more demoralizing, for the existing conditions blinded the people to spiritual values and were the direct cause of their rebellion against God.

It would be impossible to draw a picture of more widespread national depravity than the prophet has given of conditions in Judea. Every class was affected. A general spiritual apostasy was everywhere and the prophets, the spiritual leaders of the day, were proclaiming false doctrines in the name of the Lord while the priests, whose duty it was to guide the devotions of the people, were using their office for selfish purposes and to secure power and wealth.

THE PATTERN IS THE SAME

The apostasy of Jeremiah's time is reflected in our own generation in 'the unbelief which permeates the Church of Jesus Christ. Many of our ecclesiastical leaders question the miracles and belittle the inspiration of Scripture. Jeremiah's denunciation of the prophets of his day for preaching falsehoods could as readily be spoken of the preachers of today who follow the Modernist's doctrines of disbelief and the Fundamentalist's practice of spiritualizing away the literal meaning of the words of God recorded in the Bible so that the clear, definite meaning originally intended by the words used is no longer conveyed. Both schools of thought are as much in error as were the equivalent two groups in our Lord's day—the Sadducees, the Modernists of that era, and the Pharisees, the Fundamentalists of that time.

The pattern is continually being repeated, for the same causes which brought condemnation upon Judah and Jerusalem of Jeremiah's time, and later upon the Pharisees and Sadducees by John the Baptist and our Lord at the beginning of the Christian era, are also in evidence in this twentieth century. Jeremiah lamented that "the people loved to have it so." So today, preachers are more sensitive to the popular acclaim of their congregations than to their duty as servants of the Lord.

Jeremiah was not addressing the people of his time alone but prophetically he set forth the inevitability of judgment whenever apostasy rears its head. In condemning Judah of his day, Jeremiah also condemned Judah of our Lord's time, for he was looking toward the future and saw spoiler after spoiler wasting and desolating Palestine until at length, in the fullness of time, the whole country would become desolate. The first general ruin was wrought by the armies of Babylon; the final one by the armies of the Romans. Jeremiah's condemnation is therefore much greater in scope than would confine it to his generation alone. It did condemn that generation but there was also the prophetic condemnation applicable to later generations which would become as corrupt and ungodly. It is because the messages of the prophets were addressed to more than their own generations, as the seers looked down the stream of time to the end of days, that their writings are recorded in the Bible as a warning to all people everywhere of the results of unrighteousness. This is not to be taken as proof that their statements have no chronological timing. To do so is to entirely overlook the significance of Jeremiah's purpose when he paused in the midst of denouncing Judah for her sins to issue a warning to Benjamin. That tribe was informed of a time to come when a repetition of the evils of the prophet's day would again be in evidence in Judea. When that day came Benjamin was to give heed to the admonishment to flee Jerusalem and Judea.

THE WARNING TO BENJAMIN

The fact that Jeremiah's warning to Benjamin was to be heeded by that tribe at a specified time centuries later, furnishes clear evidence of the reliability of the prophetic word. It was in our Lord's day that this tribe, known then as Galileans, became the first Christians when they accepted the Messiahship of Jesus Christ. These Benjamite Galileans heeded the warning and fled Judea just before the destruction of Jerusalem by the Roman armies under Titus in 70 A.D. Jeremiah's message of warning was as follows:

"O ye children of Benjamin, gather yourselves to flee out of the midst of Jerusalem, and blow the trumpet in Tekoa, and set a sign of fire in Beth-haccerem: for evil appeareth out of the north, and great destruction." (Jer. 6: 1.)

The full significance of this warning becomes apparent when it is realized that Jeremiah turned from the
immediate task of condemning the rulers and people
of Judea to give Benjamin the sign which, if obeyed,
would preserve them to carry out their task as "light
bearers." Jesus Christ admonished His disciples to flee
when they should see armies encompass the city of
Jerusalem (Luke 21: 20-22). He did not refer to
Jeremiah's admonition; instead, he was calling His
disciples' attention to Daniel's prophecy (Matt. 24:
15). If he had cited Jeremiah, the identification of
Benjamin and their mission as "light bearers" would
have been made known, involving all that this would
imply concerning the identification of Israel, long before
God intended it should be recognized by either the
House of Israel or the Christian world. The knowledge
of Israel's identity was not to become generally known
until the time of the end.

TEKOA AND BETH-HACCEREM

What is the significance of these two places to which
Jeremiah refers? Tekoa, where the trumpet was to be
blown, stood on a projecting shoulder of the mountain
range about halfway between Jerusalem and Hebron,
and the view from it commanded nearly the whole of
Judah, with a large section of the Jordan valley. While
the site of Beth-haccerem has not been identified with
certainty, it is presumed to be the lofty conical hill a
short distance from Bethlehem. It is the most conspicu-
ous feature in the whole region. Signal fires lighted at
these two sites would arouse all Judah and thus all

Galileans in this territory would be warned as the Christians observed the signal and fled the distaster which swept over Judea.

JEREMIAH'S COMPLAINT

The prophet speaks of the uselessness of trying to arouse the people for he says they have no spirituality and will not listen to the word of the Lord. The indifference of Jeremiah's day to the things of God is repeated in every generation which turns from God and His word and apostatizes. There is in all this a striking parallel between the days of Jeremiah and modern times. Even the cry for peace, when there was no peace, so condemned by the prophet, is definitely in evidence in present day peace moves, for there can be no lasting peace apart from the adminstration of the righteousness of the laws of God. This was made clear when God called Judah to turn to the old paths and walk in the good way that they might find true peace and rest for their souls. But Judah refused to do this and so they were to reap the fruit of their evil doings for failure to hearken to His word, and because they had rejected His laws.

DROSS IN THE REFINING

It is of interest to note how often God uses the processes of refining metal to describe the methods used to purify His people. The dross, or slag, as the impurities are called today, resulting from melting and purifying metal, is the symbol of evil. The Lord declared He had set Jeremiah as an assaying tower among the people—

a building for the melting and purifying of metal. The people are referred to as grievous revolters who are in rebellion to God and whom the Lord calls "brass and iron," which evidently refers to the gray and useless alloy of copper and iron. The following process of purification is a reference to the refining of silver from baser metals by means of cupellation:

"The bellows are burned, the lead is consumed of the fire; the founder melteth in vain: for the wicked are not plucked away. Reprobate silver shall men call them, because the Lord hath rejected them." (Jer. 6: 29-30.)

This method of refining silver is to apply intense heat to vitrify the lead, which sinks into the *cupel* (a porous vessel) carrying the baser metals with it but leaving the silver in the metals in a state of purity.

Because Jerusalem was so evil, this process of refinement, applied to the city, left no pure metal but only dross. Just as Jeremiah could not find even one righteous man in the city, so no silver was secured by the above process. Jeremiah, as a refiner, depicts the state of Judah and Jerusalem as but dross which is worthless and to be discarded because of apostasy and moral depravity in evidence everywhere.

THE COMPLETION OF THE PROCESS

This same process of refining is taking place today. One cannot detect the impurities in a bar of metal until it is placed in the crucible and heat applied. In the molten state the impurities rise to the surface and the dross, or slag, is then removed, leaving the refined metal behind. This is an appropriate illustration applicable to the nations and to society today. The heat of trouble and tribulation is bringing into being evil and oppression, while men of violence are more in evidence than in former times. Such conditions have led some to believe that evil is more prevalent than in the past. Actually, the evil which has been in society is now rising to the surface, as the result of tribulation, preparatory to the day of its removal.

Such a condition of separation has been foretold for the end of the age. Jesus refers to it in the parable of the wheat and tares. (Matt. 13: 37-42.) Daniel designates the same process of separation and refinement in his statement:

"Many shall be purified, and made white, and tried; but the wicked shall do wickedly: and none of the wicked shall understand; but the wise [teachers] shall understand." (Dan. 12: 10.)

The process of refining, in which God made Jeremiah the refiner, is about to be completed in our generation when, at the return of Jesus Christ, the evil, which will have been separated from the mass of His people, will be removed from the Kingdom. A new order will then be ushered in, in which there will then be administered the laws of righteousness. Wicked men and nations will no more afflict His people "and my Holy name shall the House of Israel no more defile, neither they, nor their kings . . . and I will dwell in the midst of them for ever."

CHAPTER IV

AT THE GATE OF THE LORD'S HOUSE

The word of the Lord came to Jeremiah to stand at the gate of the Lord's House and proclaim a message to all those who entered the Temple. Jeremiah had already condemned the city of Jerusalem and its inhabitants for their sinful ways and God next instructed the prophet to proclaim a message to those who came to the Temple to worship.

Jeremiah stood at the Temple gate as commanded and called upon those who entered to mend their ways so that the Lord might cause them to dwell in safety. The people were assuming that because the Temple was in their midst He would never forsake them regardless of their evil ways. In order to impress upon them how false such reasoning really was, attention was called to Shiloh where God had first set His Name (Deut. 12:11). Jeremiah pointed out what God did to Shiloh because of the wickedness of Israel and her leaders.

THE ARK TAKEN

It was at Shiloh that the Tabernacle had been set up and there the Ark of the Covenant was kept. When Israel was being smitten before the Philistines they sent to Shiloh for the Ark which was brought into the camp of Israel. But the battle went against them and the Ark of the Lord was taken. When the news was brought to

Shiloh and Eli, the Priest, was told that the Ark had been taken and his two sons slain, the shock killed him. The report of this disaster was told to his daughter-in-law and this caused the premature birth of her child. As she lay dying, she named the child Ichabod, signifying, "The glory is departed from Israel: because the Ark of God was taken."

TEMPLE TO BECOME AS SHILOH

The Philistines apparently destroyed Shiloh though there is no specific record of the account of the disaster which befell the city. It evidently made a profound impression upon the people, evidenced in later references to it. The Psalmist gives the reason for its destruction:

"For they provoked him to anger with their high places, and moved him to jealousy with their graven images. When God heard this, he was wroth, and greatly abhorred Israel: So that he forsook the tabernacle of Shiloh, the tent which he placed among men." (Ps. 78: 58-60.)

The sins of the people, and especially of the priests employed in the Temple services, brought the curse of God upon this city and it became a desolation. Jeremiah pronounced destruction for the Temple of Solomon, declaring that it would become as Shiloh, and later added that Jerusalem would become a curse to all the nations of the earth (Jer. 26: 6). Jerusalem was finally destroyed by Nebuchadnezzar and the Temple burned, fulfilling the prophecy that it would become as Shiloh.

Later Jerusalem became a curse to all nations in the fullest sense of the word after the crucifixion of Jesus Christ and the destruction of the city by the armies of Rome in 70 A.D.

Men assumed in Jeremiah's time, and are assuming today that ritual and ceremony in religious services have magical powers like talismans to avert evil. In times of great apostasy increased emphasis invariably is placed on the observation of the ritual as the power of the Spirit declines. God has clearly demonstrated in His dealings with Israel that whether it be the Tabernacle at Shiloh, the Temple at Jerusalem or the church in modern Israel today, it is folly to expect the physical house and place where God has been reverenced to act as a guarantee against punishment when the worshippers have in their hearts turned away from God. His temple and church cannot become the refuge of ungodly men, nor will He withhold judgment merely to perpetuate an organization or protect a building from destruction because it formerly was used as a place of righteousness.

THE CHURCH TODAY

Many times church membership is mistakenly thought to denote spiritual attainment when in fact it too frequently indicates merely that names have been added to the register of organizations primarily devoted to social service. In denouncing the meaninglessness of the services in the Temple at Jerusalem, Jeremiah could as well have been speaking of conditions in many modern church services, for God's condemnation of the offerings and sacrifices in ancient Jerusalem also become a condemnation of the ritual and ceremony which in a large measure have today taken the place of true worship. Organized Christianity, holding secret and solemn assemblies, with all the accompanying pomp and ceremony, emulating the courts of an earthly monarch, is more pagan than Christian. All this is condemned by Jesus who points out its relationship to the doctrine of the Nicolaitanes * (*i.e.*, lording it over the laity), which thing He says, "I hate." It is a far cry from the simplicity of the early church and the simple services of worship and prayer. When ritual assumes precedence in religious services, the form soon becomes more sacred than the objectives of true worship, God and His Son, Jesus Christ. Men have established creeds to which they allocate more importance than the Scriptures themselves and surround their rituals with mystical and mysterious meanings without precedent for doing so in the Gospel as it is proclaimed by Jesus Christ and His disciples. Having assumed powers never granted any earthly organization, the self-appointed leaders of Christianity have resorted to a show and the appearance of holiness when the very ceremonies conducted by them proclaim the absence of the power of the Holy Spirit and a lack of true Godliness.

THE QUEEN OF HEAVEN

The people of Jerusalem had substituted the worship of the Queen of Heaven for the worship of God and

* See "What Is the Nicolaitanes' Doctrine?" By Rev. J. H. Allen, DESTINY for June 1945.

Jeremiah declared the children gathered wood and their fathers made the fires while the women made cakes to be presented to her. She was Astoreth, or Astarte, a goddess of the Phoenicians. Her worship was introduced into Israel at a very early period, and was often accompanied by immoral and lascivious rites. Her sanctuaries were generally shady groves where the votaries could practice their revelries without subjecting themselves to the public eye. Astarte represented the moon, as Baal did the sun, and her emblem was a crescent. Thus, cakes presented to her were made in the form of a crescent.

In turning from God the people were sinning against themselves for the covenant of peace that God would have made with them could not be consummated. Referring to former days, God declared He had not commanded their fathers, when He brought them out of Egypt, concerning burnt offerings, but He had commanded them to obey His voice. They were enjoined to walk in His ways and observe His laws as He had commanded that it might be well with them. However, the people refused to do so and in the stubbornness of their hearts elected to follow their own ways. He then sent His servants, the prophets, to them but they would not listen, doing worse than their ancestors.

THE PLACE OF BURNING

God forewarned Jeremiah that though he thoroughly warned the people, they were not going to heed or obey, for:

"This is a nation that obeyeth not the voice of the Lord their God, nor receiveth correction: truth is perished." (Jer. 7: 28.)

Jerusalem was addressed as a woman and commanded to cut off her hair, a practice signifying deep mourning. In the very Temple where God's name had once been held in reverence this generation had placed their abominations. They had built the high place of Tophet in the valley of Hinnom where their sons and daughters were burned in the fire in the practices of idolatrous worship.

Tophet in Aramaic means *place of burning* and is used to designate the fireplace where human beings were sacrificed, a practice widespread in antiquity. This explains Isaiah's reference to this place:

"For Tophet is ordained of old, yea, for the king it is prepared: he hath made it deep and large; the pile thereof is fire and much wood: the breath of the Lord, like a stream of brimstone, doth kindle it." (Isa. 30: 33.)

Jeremiah declared that this place of idolatry would become "the valley of slaughter" as he prophetically viewed the coming destruction which would afflict the land of Judea. This place, defiled by idols and polluted by the sacrifices of Baal and the fires of Molech, became the place of abomination, the symbol of the very gate or pit of hell. The righteous kings defiled it and threw down its altars and high places, pouring into it all the filth of the city till it became the "abhorrence" of Jerusalem.

Jesus no doubt had this place of refuse and burning in mind when he referred to the location:

"Where their worm dieth not, and the fire is not quenched." (Mark 9: 48.)

Jeremiah predicted that in the coming invasion of Palestine by the Babylonians the bones of the dead, the kings of Judah, the princes, the priests and the prophets, as well as the inhabitants, would be brought out of their graves and scattered over the ground. It is a fact of history that the invading armies vented their rage upon the dead as well as the living.

EMPTY SEPULCHRES

A vast number of the old sepulchres of Jerusalem have been explored. They are chambers hewn in the solid rock; some large and richly sculptured; some constructed with every device that could secure conceal-ment and undisturbed repose for the ashes of the illus-trious dead. But almost without exception they have been found empty. The sacrilegious plunderer has vis-ited them all, fulfilling the words of Jeremiah.*

The prophet then declares:

"The stork in the heaven knoweth her appointed times; and the turtle, and the crane, and the swallow, observe the time of their coming: but my people know not the judgment of the Lord." (Jer. 8: 7.)

Birds of the air through instinct are able to make their

---

* Some of these would also have been vacated when, "And the graves were opened; and many bodies of the saints which slept arose, and came out of the graves after his resurrection, and went into the holy city, and appeared unto many." (Matt. 27: 52-53.)

annual pilgrimages and return but men, endowed with reason and possessing revelation, neglect instruction and refuse to return to God. Jeremiah asks, how is it possible for men under such conditions to call themselves wise? Speaking of the scribes and the educated who had rejected the word of the Lord, he asks: "What can their education do for them?"

LIGHT VS. DARKNESS

This question is worthy of serious consideration today when so many are being educated in our public schools and colleges. Our theological seminaries discount God's Word and turn from its inspiration, our colleges teach the theories of evolution as fact while, with few exceptions, all our institutions of learning tend to educate young men and women away from the knowledge of the Bible.

Jesus Christ seems to have had this situation in mind when he said:

"The light of the body is the eye: if therefore thine eye be single, thy whole body shall be full of light. But if thine eye be evil, thy whole body shall be full of darkness. If therefore the light that is in thee be darkness, how great is that darkness!" (Matt. 6: 22-23.)

Ferrar Fenton translates this:

"The eye is the lamp of the body; if therefore your eye is sound, your whole body will be illuminated. But if your eye is diseased, your whole body will be in darkness. Consequently, if your sight is defective, all your body will be darkness."

In reading the above let us substitute knowledge and understanding for the word "eye." With the eye we see to select or reject. If in that process we select truth and reject error, then our mind and body will have light, but if we reverse the process, rejecting truth and selecting error, then our knowledge and understanding will be darkness as is so often the case concerning the things of the Spirit among many so-called educated persons today. Atheists and agnostics may be well educated, and may be learned men in so far as worldly wisdom is concerned; yet, because they reject God, may be in profound darkness concerning truth. The wisest man who ever lived said:

"The fear of the Lord is the beginning of wisdom: and the knowledge of the holy is understanding." (Prov. 9: 10.)

DESIRE TO ESCAPE

Jeremiah, recognizing the hopelessness of the conditions he faced, longed to escape into the wilderness to find a lodging there so that he might live apart from the people. It was a natural desire for his task of witnessing was hard and thankless. Many a man has longed to escape the responsibilities thrust upon him, especially when he must stand alone on the side of truth and face the pressure of multiplied opposition.

The message in the gate of the Temple was God's last appeal to His people and Jeremiah knew it. Though the people stray from the way and political leadership departs from righteousness, if the spiritual leadership of a nation holds firmly to the truth, the cause for alarm is greatly mitigated. In Jeremiah's day governmental and political leadership had completely failed. His present message to stir the consciences of the people and priests was a last court of appeal and also, in accord with God's warning to the prophet, foredoomed to failure. The question is asked, "Were they ashamed when they had committed abominations?" and the answer is returned, "Nay, they were not at all ashamed."

The people's defense against coming judgment was ridiculous enough but made more so by the primary reasons they gave why the inevitable punishment that Jeremiah pronounced at the direction of the Lord would not come to pass. First, they contended that the Temple of the Lord was in their midst, guaranteeing that they were God's people and immune from destruction and, secondly, they said, "The law of the Lord is with us." There is a distinctly modern ring to their contentions for it cannot be denied that during World War II our nation as a whole never for a moment considered that we could be defeated. This assumption was not based on spiritual purity and righteousness but upon the belief that because we stand before the world as a nation of churches who pay respectful homage to religious things God would protect us. The successful ending of the war but confirmed our self-righteousness, leaving a feeling of security from future alarm.

Our national failure to recognize God will require more than an outward show of righteousness and will bring suffering and trouble to us in the coming day of

His wrath. In the failure to turn to God He will be compelled through trouble and tribulation to refine us that we may serve Him in singleness of purpose. This method of compulsion is set forth by God in His answer to the prophet's lamentation. He declares He will refine His people and purge the dross out from among them, and this can only be accomplished through the fires of tribulation.

In the midst of pronouncing judgment a message is addressed to those who among His people trust in the Lord:

"Thus saith the Lord, Let not the wise man glory in his wisdom, neither let the mighty man glory in his might, let not the rich man glory in his riches: But let him that glorieth glory in this, that he understandeth and knoweth me, that I am the Lord which exercises lovingkindness, judgment and righteousness in the earth: for in these things I delight, saith the Lord." (Jer. 9: 23-24.)

Out from among every generation upon which judgment has come a remnant has escaped, for God will never forsake His covenant. When the people of His heritage stray from Him, He will, through tribulation and sorrow, compel them to return and willingly serve Him in righteousness.

CHAPTER V

THE BROKEN COVENANT

A message from the Lord in the tenth chapter of
Jeremiah, addressed to the House of Israel in captivity,
commanded them not to learn the ways of the heathen
peoples while they dwelt among them. The prophet
proceeded to analyze the idols which the heathen worshipped, giving a detailed description of the material
used in their construction. He then demonstrated how
utterly useless they are to either help themselves or
save men. "They cannot do evil," Jeremiah states,
"neither is it in them to do good." (Jer. 10: 5.)

Israel was further admonished not to be concerned
over the heavens for they were not to give heed to the
planetary houses or signs of the Zodiac. The prophet
then exclaimed:

"But the Lord is the true God, he is the living God,
and an everlasting King: at his wrath the earth shall
tremble, and the nations shall not be able to abide his
indignation. . . . He hath made the earth by his power,
he hath established the world by his wisdom." (Jer. 10:
10-12.)

JACOB'S POSITION

After pointing out how lacking in knowledge and
understanding are all those who make images which
have no life and are but the work of men's hands, for

they will perish, the prophet contrasts the position of Jacob with that of these idols:

"The portion of Jacob is not like them: for he is the former of all things; and Israel is the rod of his inheritance: the Lord of hosts is his name." (Jer. 10: 16.)

One of the difficult problems for Christians to understand is how Israel could turn from the living God and serve senseless idols modeled by men's hands. But even though Israel sinned in this way, they were not to perish like the idols which they served would finally perish. Recognizing this to be true, Jeremiah called attention to God's great promise made at the very foundation of the world concerning Israel, which Moses recorded in the following statement:

"When the Most High divided to the nations their inheritance, when he separated the sons of Adam, he set the bounds of the people according to the number of the children of Israel. For the Lord's portion is his people; Jacob is the lot [or measuring rod] of his inheritance." (Deut. 32: 8-9.)

Thus, from the very beginning, when He separated the sons of Adam, God made provision for the needs of His people Israel. It is this people whom He will use to establish the earth in righteousness for they are to occupy the promised inheritance. Now:

"The earth is the Lord's, and the fulness thereof; the world, and they that dwell therein." (Ps. 24: 1.)

So, by using Israel to establish the earth in righteousness, her "seed shall inherit the Gentiles, and make the desolate cities to be inhabited" (Isa. 54: 3).

While this promised greatness would eventually be brought to pass, God, nevertheless, was compelled to deal with His people for their rebellion against Him. Before the day arrived when Israel would come into the fullness of the covenanted blessings, both Israel and Judah must be brought, through suffering and tribulation, to a realization that Jehovah is the God of Israel. Only thus would they turn to God, forsaking their evil ways, and become willing to restore the adminstration of His laws in their land.

SIN OF UNBELIEF

For many years Jeremiah had been prophesying that trouble was coming upon Judea when Babylon would descend upon the people and carry them away into captivity. The years had rolled by and the warnings of Jeremiah had not materialized. The people and leaders were discounting all that the prophet had to say due to the apparent delay in fulfillment and they refused to believe his messages. In vain Jeremiah warned of disaster. His listeners refused to believe his message and his experience was no different than that of all the prophets, and of any man who proclaims truth distasteful to the people. Even today, when repeating the prophetic messages addressed to our generation by Jesus Christ and the prophets, the result is often indifference and disbelief. Because this was so then, the Lord declared He would "fling out the inhabitants of the land" and the distress and trouble, which they would not believe was coming, would come in accordance with

Jeremiah's prophecies and be brought home to them through actual experience.

GOD'S COVENANT

The word of the Lord came next to Jeremiah to declare the terms of His covenant to the men of Judah and the inhabitants of Jerusalem. A curse was pronounced upon anyone who refused to obey that covenant which God had made with their forefathers in the day He brought them out of the land of Egypt and from the iron furnace. This reference to "the iron furnace," while it may figuratively apply to the tribulation suffered by Israel in Egyptian bondage, can also refer to many in Israel who were condemned to work in Egyptian foundries, smelting ore to make implements of iron.

A study of the history of God's people reveals that Israel's difficulties, both in ancient and modern times, stem from the refusal to keep the terms of God's covenant. The blessings under that covenant required that Israel obey the voice of the Lord and observe and keep His commandments, statutes and judgments. If Israel would do this they would be God's people and He would be their God.

THE CONTINUING CONTROVERSY

Jeremiah informed Judah and the inhabitants of Jerusalem that if they would only obey the terms of the covenant, God would perform His oath as He swore to their forefathers. They would continue to possess the land flowing with milk and honey which they were in full possession of at that time. This message of the prophet was addressed to the people while they were still prosperous and while, as yet, the shadow of approaching calamity had not darkened the land.

The sum and substance of God's controversy with His people from the time they left Egypt to the present day is the refusal on their part to keep and observe the requirements of His covenant. In Jeremiah's time, as now, Israel stubbornly refused to obey the law with the result that the "but" clauses of the covenant began to operate. Moses set forth the terms of the "but" clauses as follows:

"But it shall come to pass, if thou wilt not hearken unto the voice of the Lord thy God, to observe to do all his commandments and his statutes which I command thee this day; that all these curses shall come upon thee, and overtake thee." (Deut. 28: 15.)

Following this statement is a long list of national troubles and calamities which eventually would end with the enemy invading the land. The people would become subject to them and deportation into another land would be the result.

Judah and Jerusalem had reached this stage in judgment because of national sins. Jeremiah was warning them that the final step in the process of judgment was at hand for failure to obey God's commands. He predicted the coming invasion would be from the north and because the sins of the people were great the only way to escape was for the nation to immediately turn to God and so he declared:

"For the Lord of hosts that planted thee hath pro-

nounced evil against thee, for the evil of the house of
Israel, and of the house of Judah, which they have done
against themselves, to provoke me to anger, in offering
incense to Baal." (Jer. 11: 17.)

A THANKLESS TASK

Regardless of the time or generation, those who bring
tidings of trouble and distress find their message an
irritation to the people who prefer to follow evil ways
which are often the easier course. It does not matter how
true the message may be, for men do not take kindly
to those who remind them of their sinful doings. Micah,
the prophet, tells of his experiences as he reports the
speech of the people whom he was warning:

"Stop it, they cry, such harping is not prophecy; no
shameful fate can e'er o'ertake the house of Jacob."
(Micah 2: 6, *Moffatt Trans.*)

This attitude furnishes the answer to the question
why Israel and Judah did not fear to sin for, though
they turned from His covenant, they believed that God
would keep His promises regarding the future greatness
of His people and would not, therefore, destroy them.
But in such reasoning the men of Israel overlooked one
important factor. While God's promises would be fulfilled, He could, did and always will punish those of
His people who turn away from Him, even though an
entire generation becomes involved in the punishment.
Because from time to time generations of His people
have failed to recognize this, and have relied for protection upon the covenant promises, the evil which they

did lost for them the blessings of peace and prosperity. These chastisements in no way militate against the ultimate fulfillment of the promised greatness, but each sinful generation so chastised has forfeited its rightful place and its blessings under the covenant.

JEREMIAH'S LIFE THREATENED

As with the rest of the prophets, so with Jeremiah, for he was no exception in that he had also won the enmity of the people because of his messages. He was a prophet of calamity as he brought home to his nation the enormity of their sins and the inevitable punishment to follow. His messages were decidedly unpopular and his very presence among them reminded the people of their sins. He declared he was innocent of the fact that they had devised mischief against him to kill him so his prophecies would not trouble them any more:

"I was like a lamb, or an ox, that is brought to the slaughter; and I knew not that they had devised devices against me, saying, Let us destroy the tree [Jeremiah] with the fruit [his prophecies] thereof, and let us cut him off from the land of the living, that his name may be no more remembered." (Jer. 11: 19.)

The prophet called for protection from them, declaring he had revealed his cause to God, for the men of Anathoth who sought his life said to him: "Prophesy not in the name of the Lord, that thou die not by our hand." The answer came from God:

"Therefore thus saith the Lord of hosts, Behold, I will punish them; the young men shall die by the sword, their sons and their daughters shall die by famine. And there shall be no remnant of them, for I will bring evil upon the men of Anathoth, even the year of their visitation." (Jer. 11: 22-23.)

This judgment was carried out in detail when the armies of Nebuchadnezzar entered the land. Those who had threatened the life of Jeremiah perished in the famine resulting from the siege of the city or died by the sword.

PROSPERITY OF THE WICKED

In every age men have asked the question, Why do the wicked prosper? The Psalmist was also concerned over this very issue. He says:

"For I was envious at the foolish, when I saw the prosperity of the wicked. . . . They are not in trouble as other men; neither are they plagued like other men. . . . Behold, these are the ungodly, who prosper in the world; they increase in riches." (Ps. 73: 3-12.)

It was not until he went into God's sanctuary that he recognized that the prosperity of evil men was but for a moment and their end would be destruction:

"Until I went into the sanctuary of God; then understood I their end." (Ps. 73: 17.)

David, too, was concerned over this issue and admonished those who were concerned over the prosperity of the wicked:

"Fret not thyself because of him who prospereth in his way, Because of the man who bringeth wicked devices to pass. . . . For evildoers shall be cut off: But those that wait upon the Lord, they shall inherit the earth. For yet a little while, and the wicked shall not be." (Ps. 37: 7-10.)

Jeremiah, the prophet, was no exception in this respect for he saw those whom he had condemned for years becoming wealthy and prospering. Because he knew God was righteous he appealed to Him and asked for permission to talk with Him concerning these things, and so he says:

"Wherefore doth the way of the wicked prosper? Wherefore are all they happy that deal very treacherously?" (Jer. 12: 1.)

He points out that the wicked are planted, take root, grow up and produce fruit, yet they only pay lip service to God while their thoughts are far from Him. Jeremiah evidently was in mental distress because of conditions in the land and God challenged him:

"If thou hast run with the footmen, and they have wearied thee, then how canst thou contend with horses? And if in the land of peace, wherein thou trustest, they weary thee, then how wilt thou do in the swelling of the Jordan?" (Jer. 12: 5.)

AN EVIL TIME

Here the prophet is reminded that if he is unable in a time of peace to face the conditions in Judea, what will he do when finally Divine wrath overflows the land? This question addressed to Jeremiah can be even more pointedly asked today as we approach the climax of the ages. If in this time of stress and perplexity, with its uncertainties concerning the immediate future, men's hearts are failing them for fear of what is coming, what will they do under the full impact of the stupendous events which are destined to accompany the great and terrible day of the Lord? Jeremiah only witnessed the beginning of judgments upon Judea and a sinful nation, while we are today witnessing a judgment whose scope is world-wide, with all nations involved as man faces the results of centuries of misrule and maladministration.

A MAN'S ENEMIES

God commands Jeremiah:

"If with your brothers, and in the house of your father, they betray you:—if they call after to seize you: —trust them not when they speak fair to you." (Jer. 12: 6, *F. F. Trans.*)

This admonition to Jeremiah is good advice to be taken in any day of distress, for often a man's enemies are those of his own household, particularly so when calamity and trouble come and his position is unpopular with the masses. In line with this warning to Jeremiah is the warning of Jesus to those who would be entrusted with the Kingdom message in the present generation, for He said: "And a man's foes shall be they of his own household" (Matt. 10: 36).

God laments the condition of His heritage and declares that the pastors have destroyed His vineyard and made the land a desolation. The prophetic sentence is pronounced that the spoilers would come for:

"The sword of the Lord shall devour from one end of the land even to the other end of the land: no flesh shall have peace . . . because of the fierce anger of the Lord." (Jer. 12: 12-13.)

A DAY OF JUDGMENT

This judgment began to be executed when the armies of Babylon over-ran Palestine and covers the intervening centuries down to modern times. Palestine has been desolated again and again with no lasting peace for its inhabitants, and even now it is a land of affliction where men live in fear, for there is no peace there. In the climax of judgment this land is to play an important part. The final phase of world conflict is about to take place there when the city of Jerusalem will be under attack according to the word of the Lord:

"Behold, I will make Jerusalem a cup of trembling unto all people round about, when they shall be in the siege both against Judah and against Jerusalem. And in that day will I make Jerusalem a burdensome stone for all people: all that burden themselves with it shall be cut in pieces, though all people of the earth be gathered together against it." (Zech. 12: 2-3.)

A TIME OF RESTORATION

God promises a restoration, not only of Israel to the land of Palestine, but of the nations, neighbors of Israel, to their own lands:

"And it shall come to pass, if they will diligently learn the ways of my people, to swear by my name, The Lord liveth; as they taught my people to swear by Baal;

then shall they be built in the midst of my people."
(Jer: 12: 16.)

Here is a call issued to the heathen peoples to turn
to God who will pardon them as He will pardon Israel.
The beginning of the fulfillment of this prophecy is
evidenced in the turning to God of multitudes of people
apart from Israel who, through the Christian missionary
activities of Israel today, have heard the Gospel. Since
the inception of missionary activities Israel has been
fulfilling her God-given mission:

"I will also give thee for a light to the Gentiles, that
thou mayest be my salvation unto the end of the earth."
(Isa. 49: 6.)

JEREMIAH IN BABYLON

In the type of a linen girdle which Jeremiah was
bidden to hide near the Euphrates, God prefigured the
coming deportation of Judah (Chapter 13). And in a
parable of bottles filled with wine he foretold the misery
and trouble in store for the inhabitants of the land.

We know from Jeremiah's record that he was acquainted with the chief leaders of Babylon, including
the King, and there is no reason to suppose, in the instructions given him to go to the River Euphrates, that
he did not visit Babylon. He would have met Daniel
who was in high favor with Nebuchadnezzar and Daniel's regard for the prophet's writings (Dan. 9: 2)
would have led him to make favorable mention of the
prophet to the King. This is borne out later in the
instructions Nebuchadnezzar gave to Nebuzar-adan, the

Captain of the Guard, to do as Jeremiah wished regarding his person (Jer. 39: 11-14). The fact that the prophet was favorably received by the King of Babylon may have accounted for the strong opposition when later he was accused of treason in advising the King of Judah, the priests and leaders, as well as the people, to give in to the demands made upon them by Nebuchadnezzar that it might be well with their nation (Jer. 27: 8-17).

The prophet used an apt illustration, often quoted because of its uniqueness. It was applicable to a people accustomed to do evil, as were Judah and the inhabitants of Jerusalem:

"Can the Ethiopian change his skin, or the leopard his spots? then may ye also do good, that are accustomed to do evil." (Jer. 13: 23.)

REASON FOR JUDGMENT

In the order of judgments to come upon Israel and Judah for national sins Moses mentions drought and famine. Jeremiah describes a grievous famine in the land, causing him to pray. But God answers him saying, "Pray not for this people," declaring:

"When they fast, I will not hear their cry; and when they offer burnt offering and an oblation, I will not accept them; but I will consume them by the sword, and by the famine, and by the pestilence." (Jer. 14: 12.)

This is in line with Solomon's remarks stating the reason why God will not answer prayer in the day of calamity:

"Because I have called, and ye refused; I have stretched out my hand, and no man regarded; But ye have set at naught all my counsel, and would none of my reproof: I also will laugh at your calamity; I will mock when your fear cometh; When your fear cometh as desolation, and your destruction cometh as a whirlwind; when distress and anguish cometh upon you.

"Then shall they call upon me, but I will not answer; they shall seek me early, but they shall not find me: For that they hated knowledge, and did not choose the fear of the Lord: They would none of my counsel: they despised all my reproof. Therefore shall they eat of the fruit of their own way, and be filled with their own devices. For the turning away of the simple shall slay them, and the prosperity of fools shall destroy them. But whoso hearkeneth unto me shall dwell safely, and shall be quiet from fear of evil." (Prov. 1: 24-33.)

FALSE TEACHERS REPUDIATED

Jeremiah reminded the Lord that even the prophets were telling the people in His name that sword and famine would not afflict the land and were assuring them that they would have continued peace. God replied:

"The prophets prophesy lies in my name; I sent them not, neither have I commanded them, neither spake unto them: they prophesy unto you a false vision and divination, and a thing of naught, and the deceit of their hearts." (Jer. 14: 14.)

In this fearful denunciation of the spiritual leaders of Jeremiah's time is the denunciation of all those who

purport to speak in the name of the Lord in every age
but who disbelieve God and refuse to give heed to His
Word. God has not sent them, nor can they truly speak
for Him when they belittle His Word and refuse to
accept the divine revelation of God's purposes regarding
man. And so judgment is pronounced upon these false
leaders:

"Therefore thus saith the Lord concerning the prophets [preachers] that prophesy [preach] in my name,
and I sent them not, yet they say, Sword and famine
shall not be in this land; by sword and famine shall
these prophets be consumed." (Jer. 14: 15.)

The people to whom they preached could not use
these false teachings as an excuse, for they also were
guilty. It is evident that Jeremiah had borne sufficient
witness among them so that, in spite of erroneous teaching from false teachers, the people had been sufficiently
warned of the evil to come that they were accountable
for their own sins. God commanded the prophet to stand
in the sight of the people and bewail the coming
calamities.

JUDAH FOLLOWS ISRAEL

A situation similar to that which confronted Jeremiah
preceded the deportation of the House of Israel into
Assyria. The judgment pronounced upon Israel was for
the same trespasses as were now being committed by
Judah. Judea and the inhabitants of Jerusalem knew all
this, yet they persisted in their evil ways and provoked
God to anger against them. The record of Israel's sins

and her deportation is given in II Kings 17 where it is stated:

"For so it was, that the children of Israel had sinned against the Lord their God. . . . And walked in the statutes of the heathen. . . . And the children of Israel did secretly those things that were not right against the Lord their God. . . . And they set them up images and groves in every high hill . . . they rejected his statutes, and his covenant that he made with their fathers, and his testimonies which he testified against them; and they followed vanity, and became vain. . . . And they left all the commandments of the Lord their God. . . . Therefore the Lord was very angry with Israel, and removed them out of his sight: there was none left but the tribe of Judah only. Also Judah kept not the commandments of the Lord their God, but walked in the statutes of Israel which they made." (II Kings 17: 7-19.)

Judah had now come to judgment and, some one hundred and thirty years after Israel was taken captive to Assyria, Jeremiah proclaimed the fact that Judah was at the point of being carried away into Babylonian captivity for the same major sins that the House of Israel had committed before her—the refusal to obey God's covenant.

CHAPTER VI

THE CALL FOR FISHERS AND HUNTERS

Because the people of Judah and the inhabitants of Jerusalem had passed beyond any possibility of listening to reason and reproof and were not ashamed of their evil ways, having despised and rejected the word of God, the Lord declared:

"Though Moses and Samuel stood before me, yet my mind could not be toward this people; cast them out of my sight, and let them go forth." (Jer. 15: 1.)

This is an interesting allusion to the time that both Moses and Samuel interceded for Israel and God listended to them and spared the nation. When Moses returned from the Mount with the two tables of stone on which God's law was written he found the people worshipping the Golden Calf and indulging in licentious practices. Moses recognized the great sin that was being committed and broke the tables of stone. Later he charged the people:

"Ye have sined a great sin: and now I will go up unto the Lord; peradventure I shall make an atonement for your sin. And Moses returned unto the Lord, and said, Oh, this people have sinned a great sin, and have made them gods of gold. Yet now, if thou wilt forgive their sin —; and if not, blot me, I pray thee, out of thy book which thou hast written." (Ex. 32: 30-32.)

God listened to Moses, declaring that only those who

had sinned against Him would be blotted out of His book. He instructed Moses:

"Therefore now go, lead the people unto the place of which I have spoken unto thee: behold, mine Angel shall go before thee: nevertheless in the day when I visit I will visit their sin upon them. And the Lord plagued the people, because they made the calf, which Aaron made." (Ex. 32: 34-35.)

PROVOKING GOD

Again, at the border of the promised land, Israel murmured against Moses and Aaron for, after listening to the reports of the spies who had been sent over to spy out the land of Palestine, they said:

"Would God that we had died in the land of Egypt! or would God we had died in this wilderness. And wherefore hath the Lord brought us unto this land, to fall by the sword, that our wives and our children should be a prey? were it not better for us to return into Egypt?" (Num. 14: 2-3.)

Only two out of the twelve spies sent out returned with a favorable report. These two were Joshua and Caleb who declared that if God delighted in His people He would give them victory over their enemies. But the people would not listen and rose up against the men to stone them. Then the glory of the Lord appeared in the Tabernacle and the Lord said to Moses:

"How long will this people provoke me? and how long will it be ere they believe me, for all the signs which I have shewed among them? I will smite them with the pestilence, and disinherit them, and will make of thee a great nation and mightier than they." (Numbers 14: 11-12.)

Moses again interceded in behalf of the people and earnestly prayed the Lord to have mercy and forgive their iniquity and trespasses:

"Pardon, I beseech thee, the iniquity of this people according unto the greatness of thy mercy, and as thou hast forgiven this people, from Egypt even until now. And the Lord said, I have pardoned according to thy word." (Num. 14: 19-20.)

PHILISTINES DEFEATED

Samuel experienced a similar situation during his judgeship. After the Ark of the Covenant had been returned to Israel by the Philistines it rested for many years in Kirjathjearim.* The people were mourning because of their sins and Samuel spoke to them, reminding them that if they would return to the Lord with all their hearts and put away the strange gods and serve the Lord, and Him only, He would deliver them from the hands of the Philistines.

Samuel gathered all Israel to Mizpeh where he prayed for them. There he offered a sacrifice and the people acknowledged their sins. It was a time of great revival in Israel. But when the Philistines heard of the gathering at Mizpeh they moved against them. Samuel interceded with the Lord for Israel and the Lord hearkened:

* See Chapter IV, "At the Gate of the Lord's House," page 46.

"And as Samuel was offering up the burnt offering, the Philistines drew near to battle against Israel: but the Lord thundered with a great thunder [or roar] on that day upon the Philistines, and discomfited them; and they were smitten before Israel." (I Sam. 7: 10.)

JUDGMENT PRONOUNCED

The Psalmist refers to both Moses and Samuel as having power and influence with God (Ps. 99: 6-7) but Judah's sins had become so great and the people so hardened in their evil ways that God informed Jeremiah that, though Moses and Samuel were present to plead for them, it would not avail. Therefore, the Lord said they were to go forth, but when Jeremiah was asked, no doubt in sarcasm by the leaders and people who had long ago ceased to take his prophecies seriously, "Whither shall we go?" he replied:

"Thus saith the Lord; Such as are for death, to death; and such as are for the sword, to the sword; and such as are for the famine, to the famine; and such as are for the captivity, to the captivity. And I will appoint over them four kinds [families], saith the Lord; the sword to slay, and the dogs to tear, and the fowls of the heaven, and the beasts of the earth, to devour and destroy. And I will cause them to be removed into all kingdoms of the earth." (Jer. 15: 2-4.)

This prophecy has been literally fulfilled and no atheist or agnostic can honestly deny the fact for many of the descendants of Judah are without a country of their own, scattered over the face of the earth, residing upon every continent and among all nations. Today, under an awakening desire to again become a nation and possess the land of Palestine, the Jews are actively interested in securing sole rulership over the land which belongs to all Israel. They have forgotten that in the days of Jeremiah the cause of their banishment was disbelief in God and their troubles today result from their refusal to believe in His Son, Jesus Christ, who is Lord and Saviour.

A CRY OF DESPAIR

Recognizing the fast approaching trouble soon to engulf his people, Jeremiah lamented:

"Woe is me, my mother, that thou has borne me a man of strife and a man of contention to the whole earth!" (Jer. 15: 10.)

Jeremiah pleaded in his own defense that he was a righteous man who kept the law. In the Israel concept the meanest type of man was he who lent and borrowed upon usury (putting one's money out to interest) for this is contrary to the law of the Lord. Jeremiah complained because he was cursed by the people as though he were such a man. When God commissioned Jeremiah for his mission the prophet was informed that he was to be as a defenced city against the kings of Judah, the princes, the priests and the people. Though they would fight against him the Lord promised:

"They shall not prevail against thee; for I am with thee, saith the Lord, to deliver thee." (Jer. 1: 19.)

Jeremiah recalled this promise that the enemy would

treat him well in the time of affliction and the prophet considered he was already in a time of affliction, for those of his own people who had become his enemies were certainly not treating him well. The prophet knew Judah would not be able to withstand the onslaught of her enemies, but it also seemed to him that he would be vanquished himself by the evil treachery of his people and this was contrary to God's promise that he would be a fortress of strength against them.

That Judah would fall before the armies of Babylon is indicated in the statement: "Shall iron [Judah] break the northern iron and steel [Babylon]?" The Hebrew word *Nechushah* translated *steel* in this passage should have been rendered *copper*. In ancient times copper was mixed with other metals to render it hard and durable. Also northern iron was of a more superior quality and more nearly like our steel and a method of hardening this iron was known at a very early period in history.

A DISCOURAGED PROPHET

Jeremiah, concerned over the pressure under which he lived, prayed:

"O Lord, thou knowest: remember me, and visit me, and revenge me of my persecutors." (Jer. 15: 15.)

Continuing, the prophet reminded the Lord that he suffered rebuke for His sake. He had found and embraced God's words which were sweet and pleasant to him but because of the stand he had taken he was derisively labeled a prophet and subject to continued per-

secution. Jeremiah referred to the fact that he had never
joined the assembly of the revelers or merry-makers
but instead he sat alone because of the task God had
assigned him. It was his lot to endure all kinds of in-
dignities from those whom he had been commissioned
to warn and because this was so the prophet said his
torment was like the perpetual pain of an incurable
wound. His despair led him to question the Lord:

"Wilt thou really disappoint me, like a stream that
runs dry?" (Jer. 15: 18, *Moffatt Trans.*)

Under the pressure of loneliness the prophet, in a
moment of complete discouragement, questioned the
fulfillment of the messages God had directed him to
declare to Judah. For years he had been prophesying
of disaster to come but the delay in fulfillment had
made him an object of mockery. As a result he had
reached the limit of his endurance and murmured
against the Lord to the extent that he stood in danger
of being dismissed from service as a prophet of God.

GOD'S REPLY

God called upon Jeremiah to return to Him and cease
his murmurings in order to be reinstated as His spokes-
man, but He gave the prophet no assurance whatever
of relief from pressure. Patience was the paramount
requirement in waiting, for the verdict of time would
finally bring full justification.

The Lord informed Jeremiah he was not to go to the
people any more. That phase of his mission was completed. From that time on he was to wait and let the

people come to him, for those who had refused to listen in the past would, under pressure of coming evil conditions, be compelled to eventually turn to him for guidance and assistance. God warned the prophet, however, that when they did come he must be discreet and pick from among the unrepentant the remnant who, with him, and because of him, would be treated well by the enemy. God promised:

"I will deliver you from evil men, and free you from the clutches of the cruel." (Jer. 15: 21, *Moffatt Trans.*)

FORBIDDEN TO MARRY

Jeremiah was forbidden to take a wife and have sons and daughters in that place. He was to refrain from attending funerals or going to the places of mourning and also to abstain from attending feasts or marriage festivals because in his day all this would cease in the utter ruin to overtake the land. The predicted captivity, long delayed, was about to begin.

PROMISED RESTORATION

In the midst of predicting calamity and the deportation of Judah to another land the word of the Lord came to Jeremiah concerning the promised restoration of the House of Israel:

"Therefore, behold, the days come, saith the Lord, that it shall no more be said, The Lord liveth that brought up the children of Israel out of the land of Egypt; But, The Lord liveth that brought up the children of Israel from the land of the north, and from all lands whither he had driven them: and I will bring them again into their land that I   gave unto their fathers." (Jer. 16: 14-15.)

The discouraged prophet was encouraged by God who gave him a message of hope concerning the future restoration of Israel. That this prophecy has to do mainly with the House of Israel, and not the Jews who came from the House of Judah, is clearly indicated by the mission assigned to the fishers and hunters and by its fulfillment in the Christian Dispensation.

FISHERS AND HUNTERS

The Lord sets forth the method by which He will bring Israel back to Himself. This is a most important prophecy for in sending for fishers and hunters the way in which Israel is to be awakened to spiritual values and to the need of obeying His Covenant is revealed to Jeremiah:

"Behold, I will send for many fishers, saith the Lord, and they shall fish them; and after will I send for many hunters, and they shall hunt them from every mountain, and from every hill, and out of the holes of the rocks." (Jer. 16: 16.)

Who are these fishers and hunters and what is the particular task each is to perform in the respective fishing and hunting periods? The sending of these two groups designated as fishers and hunters indicates that there are two entirely different methods by which an appeal would be made to Israel. A fisherman patiently waits as he undertakes to snare the fish in a net or catch it on a line, but the hunter tramps through the woods and over the hills and mountains exerting energy and strength as he travels in search of his especially selected prey. Actually Jeremiah prophetically referred to the two distinct phases of the Gospel in their respective appeals to Israel for the purpose of bringing them back to covenant relationship with God. The first would require fishers and the period of their fishing is clearly defined by the events of the Gospel Age. The second would require hunters and the period of their activity would be at the end of the Gospel Age. This is demonstrated by the activities of those who have sought to establish the identity of Israel in these last days, hunting out the evidence and tracing Israel from Palestine throughout her years of wanderings to the present time. History reveals how faithfully the predicted fishing and hunting missions have been carried out by those chosen of God for each purpose.

THE FISHERS

Let us first deal with the evidence demonstrating that God did send for many fishers who proclaimed the glad tidings of salvation. This portion of Jeremiah's prophecy began to be fulfilled when Jesus Christ came and selected His disciples, constituting them fishers of men:

"And Jesus, walking by the sea of Galilee, saw two brethren, Simon called Peter, and Andrew his brother, casting a net into the sea: for they were fishers. And he saith unto them, Follow me, and I will make you fishers of men." (Matt. 4: 18-19.)

Throughout the centuries of the Dispensation of

Grace the disciples and followers of our Lord have been proclaiming the Gospel of salvation by which Israel would be brought into New Covenant relationship with her God. Jeremiah later refers to this New Covenant to be made with the House of Israel (Jer. 31: 31-33) and, in commissioning His disciples to proclaim the Gospel, Jesus sent them to the lost sheep of the House of Israel (Matt. 10: 6).

Because the Nation of the Jews rejected Jesus Christ and His teachings, provision was made for the transfer of the Kingdom, which He declared would be taken from them and given to a nation willing and able to accept the attending responsibilities. Jesus said to the Pharisees and Chief Priests:

"Therefore say I unto you, The kingdom of God shall be taken from you, and given to a nation bringing forth the fruits thereof." (Matt. 21: 43.)

The task of making that transfer was assigned to the followers of our Lord. Abundant evidence from secular sources exists concerning the establishment of the first Christian Church in the Isles by Joseph of Arimathea when the little Wattle Church was built at Glastonbury, England only a few years after the crucifixion. The same evidence points to the coming of Saint Paul who, on one of his missionary journeys to London, preached the Gospel from Ludgate Hill. The fact is that the Lord God of Israel, who called His people to be His servants, saw to it that they received their commission first hand. So, by the hand of His disciples and early followers, Jesus Christ sent the Gospel directly to the

Isles in the process of transferring to Israel abroad the blessings of salvation and the knowledge of the Kingdom.

BENJAMIN'S MISSION

The question naturally arises, what actually was taken from the Jews? After they returned from the Babylonian captivity they never again became a kingdom and until the coming of the Lord remained but a nation only without a king. Let us briefly review the facts. Because of Solomon's sins he was told the Kingdom would be taken from him; nevertheless, it would not be entirely removed, for, through the prophet, God said:

"Howbeit I will not rend away all the kingdom; but will give one tribe to thy son for David my servant's sake, and for Jerusalem's sake." (I King's 11: 13.)

Benjamin, one of the Israel tribes, was left which meant that a Kingdom tribe remained with Judah. When the House of Israel was taken captive to Assyria for her sins Benjamin was not involved, nor was this tribe numbered among the tribes of Israel whom God divorced for their idolatry. When the House of Israel became "not God's people" (see Hosea 1: 9) the tribe of Benjamin was still His Kingdom people. The Galileans of our Lord's Day were Benjamites and it was from this tribe that Jesus chose His disciples * and constituted them "fishers of men," declaring they would be "the light of the world".

* See "Divine Selections and Rejections, DESTINY, October, 1944.

When at the last the Jews rejected Jesus Christ and turned against the early disciples, who were Galileans and of the tribe of Benjamin with the one exception, Judas Iscariot, the brotherhood between Judah and Israel was broken (Zech. 11:14). That brotherhood could exist only as long as Benjamin and Judah were united. The Galileans, with others of the early Christians, heeded the warning given by Jeremiah * and fled Judea just before the seige of Jerusalem by Titus, the Roman general.

Judah lost the Kingdom by the refusal to accept Jesus Christ and the departure of the tribe of Benjamin who, as Christians, became fishers to fish for Israel, fulfilled our Lord's words to the Jews that the Kingdom would be taken from them. The "light-bearers" left Palestine and the transfer of the Kingdom to a nation bringing forth the fruits thereof came as the result of Benjamin moving toward the west, following in the wake of the westward trek of their brethren of Israel. Arriving in the Isles, they began to "fish" for Israel and the message of redemption and salvation was received by Israel dwelling in the islands. In the process of time the Anglo-Saxon-Celtic peoples (modern Israel) accepted Christianity as the result of the work of those sent to fish for them.

THE HUNTERS

The fishers were to be followed by many hunters according to Jeremiah, thus indicating a change in method

* See Chapter III, "God's Controversy with Judah," page 41.

and message. The task of the hunters was to *search* for Israel. The fisherman blindly casts his net and gathers into it all kinds of fish, some good and some bad. That is not so with the hunter who seeks to find the particular object of his search. All this points to the modern endeavor to identify the House of Israel in the world today. It has been a painstaking matter of research, comparing the records of the past with the marks by which the race was to be identified in the latter days. The history of nations and peoples and the migration of races have all been carefully checked until, finally, the identity of the people who are modern Israel has been established. All this has been on date and on time according to God's plan.

The hunting process has been intensified during the present generation and has resulted in volumes of evidence being adduced to clearly demonstrate that the Anglo-Saxon-Celtic peoples are the House of Israel today. This identification has been immediately followed by the need of proclaiming the responsibility of this race to obey the Covenant God made with their forefathers. This is the Gospel of the Kingdom which is to be proclaimed just before the age ends. Concerning the preaching of this Gospel Jesus said:

"Ye shall not have gone over the cities of Israel, till the Son of man be come." (Matt. 10: 23.)

Now the cities of Israel have heard the voice of the fishers who have not only proclaimed the gospel of salvation in every city, hamlet and town in the Israel lands but have also carried the knowledge of salvation

to the ends of the earth. But the Gospel of the Kingdom was to be proclaimed exclusively to the Israel
peoples. All the cities and towns in the Israel lands have
not yet heard this message which the hunters have been
commissioned to proclaim. This gospel is, however,
going out in an ever increasing volume and of it Jesus
said:

"The good news of the Kingdom, however, shall be
proclaimed throughout the whole Empire, as a witness
to all nations; and then the end will come." (Matt. 24:
14, *F. F. Trans.*)

And so in conformity with Isaiah's prophecy the call
is going out to modern Israel:

"Hearken to me, ye that follow after righteousness,
ye that seek the Lord: look unto the rock whence ye are
hewn, and to the hole of the pit whence ye are digged.
Look unto Abraham your father, and unto Sarah that
bare you." (Isa. 51: 1-2.)

The hunters have been searching and as they search
the call is continually going out to Israel to awaken to
the knowledge of their Israelitish identity and to the
fact that Abraham is their father and they are the sons
of Isaac, i.e., *I-Sac-Sons*, or Saxons. With this call the
national phase of the Gospel of the Kingdom is going
out in ever increasing volume, for in the light of the
knowledge of their identity Israel must restore the
administration of His commandments, statutes and
judgments that justice and equity may be established
in the land:

"Thus saith the Lord, Keep ye judgment, and do

justice: for my salvation is near to come, and my righteousness to be revealed." (Isa. 56: 1.)

The task of the hunters is augmented by the need to declare Israel's national sins, calling upon her to return to the Lord and comply with all the requirements of His Covenant. So the instruction continues:

"Cry aloud, spare not, lift up thy voice like a trumpet, and shew my people their transgression, and the house of Jacob their sins." (Isa. 58: 1.)

Though the people of Israel have been lost to the world as far as their identity is concerned, they have never been lost to God for He watched over and led them through all their wanderings to the appointed place, even while they were under the curse of having broken His Covenant:

"For mine eyes are upon all their ways: they are not hid from my face, neither is their iniquity hid from mine eyes." (Jer. 16: 17.)

Because the time was long and many years would transpire before the day of restoration, the Lord informed Jeremiah that during this period Israel must first expiate their sins:

"First I will recompense their iniquity and their sins double; because they have defiled my land, they have filled mine inheritance with the carcases of their detestable and abominable things." (Jer. 16: 18.)

The history of the long seven times of punishment for both Israel and Judah because of their sins has proved how truly this judgment has been visited upon them for their disobedience to God, to His word and to His Laws.

The purpose of this long period of punishment, with the events which will climax in the "Time of Jacob's Trouble" as the age ends and the time of the restoration of the Kingdom comes, is set forth by the Lord:

"So I will let them feel, this once I will let them feel, the full force of my power, to teach them that my name is the Eternal." (Jer. 16: 21 *Moffatt Trans.*)

HOPE FOR THE GENTILES

One of the major results to follow as an outcome of the fishing for Israel is to be the gathering in of multitudes who are not of Israel. This will come as the proclamation of the Gospel of Salvation reaches to the ends of the earth. The prophet voices the question of the Gentiles by which they confess their need of the one true God:

"O thou Eternal, my strength, my stronghold, my refuge in the hour of trouble, nations shall come from the ends of the earth to thee, saying, All the traditions our fathers inherited were lies, vain and profitless. Is a man to make gods for himself—gods that are no gods at all?" (Jer. 16: 19-20. *Moffat Trans.*)

Thus in bringing the knowledge of salvation to Israel the way is opened for the Gentiles to accept Jesus Christ as their Saviour, giving to them, with Israel, a right to citizenship in the Kingdom and a share in its blessings.

CHAPTER VII

JEREMIAH AT THE POTTER'S HOUSE

The incurability of the sins of Judah is fittingly described by the following simile:

"The sin of Judah is written with a pen of iron, and with the point of a diamond: it is graven upon the table of their heart, and upon the horns of your altars." (Jer. 17: 1.)

So indelibly written upon the hearts of the people of Judah was the propensity to idolatry, evidenced by their many altars to heathen deities, that the people were beyond hope of repentance. For this reason God declared they would serve their enemies in a foreign land.

THE UNGODLY AND GODLY

Jeremiah drew a contrast between those who trust in man, having turned away from God, and those who rely upon Him in whom they put their trust. A curse is pronounced upon the man who puts his trust in mankind alone. He is likened to a desert scrub that never thrives because it lives in a dry place and endures the scorching heat of the desert and barren land that cannot be inhabited.

A blessing is pronounced upon the man who puts his trust in the Lord for he is likened to a tree planted beside a stream whose roots are well watered. No drought can affect it and such a tree is untouched by any fear of scorching heat. Its leaves are ever green and it bears fruit even in times of distress.

This contrast between the ungodly and the Godly is as apt today as it was in Jeremiah's time for, modern concepts to the contrary notwithstanding, man will never arrive at a stage in the progress of civilization where he can do without God. Only the man who fully trusts in the Lord can be serene and content in a time of trouble and distress. Those who do not know the Lord are apprehensive, worried and concerned for their personal security and safety. The Psalmist has succinctly summarized this contrast between the Godly and the ungodly:

"Blessed is the man that walketh not in the counsel of the ungodly, nor standeth in the way of sinners, nor sitteth in the seat of the scornful. But his delight is in the law of the Lord; and in his law doth he meditate day and night. And he shall be like a tree planted by the rivers of water, that bringeth forth his fruit in his season; his leaf also shall not wither; and whatsoever he doeth shall prosper.

"The ungodly are not so: but are like the chaff which the wind driveth away. Therefore the ungodly shall not stand in the judgment, nor sinners in the congregation of the righteous. For the Lord knoweth the way of the righteous: but the way of the ungodly shall perish." (Ps. 1: 1-6.)

MEN ACCOUNTABLE TO GOD

One of the clear teachings of Scripture is that men must finally give an account before God of the deeds committed in the flesh. That no man can escape this judgment is clear from the following pronouncement of the Lord:

"The heart is deceitful above all things, and desperately wicked: who can know it? I the Lord search the heart, I try the reins, even to give every man according to his ways, and according to the fruit of his doings." (Jer. 17: 9-10.)

Moffatt renders this:

"Deep is a man's mind, deeper than all else, on evil bent; who can fathom it? I the Eternal search the mind, I test the heart, rewarding every man as he has lived, and as his deeds deserve."

LOVE OF MONEY

Man's material possessions are next taken into consideration. Paul declared that we have brought nothing into the world and it is certain we can carry nothing out, and so he said:

"Having food and raiment let us be therefore content. But they that will be rich fall into temptation and a snare, and into many foolish and hurtful lusts, which drown men in destruction and perdition. For the love of money is the root of all evil." (I Tim. 6: 8-10.)

The apostle did not say that money is the root of evil but that it is the *love* of it which is the root of all evil. The love of money and the power its possession brings have been the foundation of evil in every generation and countless numbers of men have sold their souls and a right to a spiritual heritage for money. These conditions were extant in Jeremiah's time and the prophet pronounces those fools who have made money by unfair means:

"As the bird hatches what she laid not,
He who by unjustice makes wealth,
In the midst of his days he may lose,
And at the last be regarded a fool!"

Jer. 17:11, *F. F. Trans.*)

Jesus Christ clearly set forth the foolishness of those who strive for things which perish:

"For what is a man profited, if he shall gain the whole world, and lose his own soul? or what shall a man give in exchange for his soul?" (Matt. 16:26.)

And so Paul advises those who are blessed with wealth:

"To the rich in the present age I advise not to think too highly, nor to trust upon an uncertain wealth; but upon God who has prepared for us all wealth for enjoyment; to do good, to enrich themselves with good deeds, to be liberal, affable, and to lay up for themselves a noble foundation for the future, so that they may acquire the enduring life." (I Tim. 6:17-19, *F. F. Trans.*)

JUDGMENT FOR UNRIGHTEOUSNESS

The final judgment for the unrighteous is as follows:

"A glorious high throne from the beginning is the place of our sanctuary. O Lord, the hope of Israel, all that forsake thee shall be ashamed, and they that depart from me shall be written [debased] in the earth, because they have forsaken the Lord, the fountain of living waters." (Jer. 17: 12-13.)

Jeremiah complained of the sneers and taunts of the people as they challenged him to show them where the calamities were which he had been continually predicting. The prophet reminded the Lord that he had been a faithful pastor and had not pressed Him for fulfillment of His word nor longed for the day of judgment. The difficulties and troubles which he had proclaimed would come upon the people had in a measure come upon the prophet himself. So he asked the Lord to let those who tormented him be terrified and bring upon them the day of evil with double destruction. This is another glimpse of the human side of this prophet for it was the cry of a man who saw the wicked prospering around him while he suffered at their hands for declaring the truth as God had required. It was his day of trouble so he asked the Lord not to be a terror to him but instead a refuge from the evil day.

AT THE CITY GATE

Jeremiah was then commanded to stand in the gate of the city (Moffatt states this was the Gate of Benjamin) where the kings of Judah passed in and out of the city. The gates of a city were places of assembly where often public markets were established, and particularly they were places of legal tribunals.

A seat "among the elders" in the gates (Prov. 31:23) was a high honor while "oppression in the gates" indicated corruption in administration (Prov. 22: 22; Isa. 29: 21). The King at times held special public audiences in the gate (II Sam. 19: 8). The prophets and teachers went to the gates with their messages, since they were the places where the throngs gathered (I Kings 22: 10). The city's gates were also a place where the debased and drunkards congregated as well (Ps. 69: 12).

SABBATH OBSERVANCE

Evidently the gate used by the Kings of Judah was the most popular gathering place for the inhabitants of Jerusalem and it was there that Jeremiah went in response to the Lord's command. The prophet addressed his message to the throngs gathered there admonishing them to take heed that they bear no burden or engage in trading on the Sabbath day; nor should they bring loads of any kind either from their homes within the city or from the country without to the gates on the day of rest. The people were reminded that on that day they were to do no work as God had instructed their fathers.

The promise was made that if the people of Judea and the inhabitants of Jerusalem would listen to the warning and refrain from bringing goods to the gates of the city on the day of rest, sanctifying the Sabbath day and keeping from doing any business on that day:

"Then shall there enter into the gates of this city kings and princes sitting upon the throne of David, riding in chariots and on horses, they, and their princes, the men of Judah, and the inhabitants of Jerusalem; and this city shall remain forever." (Jer. 17: 25.)

Jeremiah declared that if the Sabbath was kept holy Jerusalem would remain a city inhabited in peace forever. There the people would come from the villages of Judah and from the suburbs of Jerusalem, from the land of Benjamin, from the slopes, the hills and the deserts, bringing their tithes and gathering to worship in the Temple of the Lord. But if they refused to keep the Sabbath holy, the alternative to these blessings was as follows:

"But if ye will not hearken unto me to hallow the sabbath day, and not to bear a burden, even entering in at the gates of Jerusalem on the sabbath day; then will I kindle a fire in the gates thereof, and it shall devour the palaces of Jerusalem, and it shall not be quenched." (Jer. 17: 27.)

BAROMETER OF SPIRITUALITY

Why does the Lord lay so much stress upon the need of keeping a Sabbath of rest sacred unto Him? It is because the attitude of the people toward the observance of the Sabbath is a perfect barometer of their spirituality:

"Setting aside one day in seven as holy unto the Lord was to be a sign between Israel and God forever. Those who failed to keep this law were to be put to death. Those who worked on that day were to be cut off from among His people. This judgment may seem severe, but let us remember the fulfillment of or failure to keep this law was a perfect barometer of the spirituality of His people. When the nation turns from its God the very first indication is recognized by their attitude towards the Sabbath day. It is interesting to note that in identically the same ratio as our nation sinks into a state of spiritual decadency, so have we increased the desecration of the Sabbath day. Instead of a Holy Day it has become a holiday and for this our entire nation suffers." (*Digest of the Divine Law*, page 59.)

THE DAY

This raises the question *which day?* inasmuch as some claim Saturday rather than Sunday should be observed as the day of rest. A full discussion of this subject will be found in *Digest of the Divine Law*, pages 59 to 62, from which the following is taken:

"We are not concerned with the controversy over a day on which much has already been written by both groups in their endeavor to prove that the particular day which they keep is the only true observance of the law. The law requires that one day in seven be set aside as holy. In the spirit of this law both Jew and Christian are observing its requirements if, following the six days of labor, they rest on the seventh."

READY FOR JUDGMENT

When Israel and Judah turned completely away from observing the law of the Sabbath, to keep the day holy, the end of prosperity and peace came. What was true then is true now for when God's people finally refuse to hallow the Sabbath judgment is imminent.

Tried by the standards which God set for the observance of His Holy Day, the world at large, and Israel particularly, is overdue for judgment today. We have turned the Sabbath of rest into a day of profit and pleasure. Jeremiah's condemnation of his generation is also a condemnation of this 20th century generation to whom Isaiah the prophet has addressed the following message:

"If on Sabbath you hold back your foot,
And make My Holy Day your delight,
And declare that My rest is a pleasure,
To worship the Lord with respect,
And by forming your path do it honour,
Not seeking your pleasure or trade.
Thus delighting yourself with the Lord,
You shall ride on the Heights of the Earth,
And feed on the portion of Jacob, your father,—
So the Lord's mouth has declared!"

(Isa. 58: 13-14 *F. F. Trans.*)

The importance of keeping one seventh of our time set apart for the Lord is great in His sight if we are to expect continued prosperity as it is important to personal blessing in the work of our hands to give Him a tenth of our increase.

THE CLAY VESSEL

God next instructed Jeremiah to go down to a potter's house. The prophet obeyed the command and there he found the potter working upon a vessel on the wheels.

The shaping of vessels on the wheels dates back to

very early history. In their original form the wheels were stone disks arranged to be turned by hand on a vertical axis. The wheels used in Palestine and Syria today probably differ in no respect from those used in Jeremiah's time. The wheel or, to be more exact, the wheels, are fitted on a square wooden or iron shaft about three feet long. The lower disk is about 20 inches in diameter, and the upper one 8 to 12 inches in diameter. The lower end of the shaft is pointed and fits into a stone socket or bearing in which it rotates. A second bearing just below the upper disk is so arranged that the shaft inclines slightly away from the potter. The potter leans against a slanting seat, bracing himself with one foot so that he will not slide off, and with the sole of his other foot he kicks the upper face of the lower wheel, thus making the whole machine rotate. The lower wheel is often of stone to give greater momentum. With a marvelous dexterity, which a novice tries in vain to imitate, he gives the pieces of clay on the upper wheel any shape he desires.

Jeremiah watched the potter at work moulding the clay upon the wheel and the vessel he was making was spoiled in his hands so he remoulded it until he was satisfied.

THE DIVINE POTTER

The word of the Lord came to Jeremiah saying:

"O house of Israel, cannot I do with you as this potter? saith the Lord. Behold, as the clay is in the potter's hands, so are ye in mine hand, O house of Israel." (Jer. 18: 6.)

Now the House of Israel was in exile and away from Palestine as a result of the Assyrian invasions and captivity. They had been living in the land of their captors for over a hundred years at the time Jeremiah was speaking.

THE BROKEN BOTTLE

In contrast with the illustration of the House of Israel the condition of the House of Judah was depicted in the command to Jeremiah to get a potter's earthen bottle (fired pottery) with which he was to demonstrate the judgment upon Judah. Jeremiah was told to take with him some of the leaders among the people and the priests and go to the valley opposite the pottery-gate where he was to proclaim a message of judgment upon them for their evil ways. He was then to break the bottle in the sight of those who went with him and say to them:

"Thus saith the Lord of hosts: Even so will I break this people and this city, as one breaketh a potter's vessel, that cannot be made whole again." (Jer. 19: 11.)

The captivity of Judah was imminent for, together with Benjamin, a tribe of Israel, they were about to be carried away into Babylonian captivity. We know the fate of the House of Judah for nationally they were broken and after 70 A.D., ceased to be a nation any more. Also, as a result of the rejection of Jesus Christ, the breach between Judah and Israel was completed for, with Benjamin Christianized, the brotherhood was broken as predicted by the prophet (Zech. 11:14).

TWO DISTINCT PEOPLES

The House of Israel was the vessel of clay damaged in the making but still workable clay capable of being reshaped. But the House of Judah was the earthen vessel, already formed and baked in the fire, then broken in pieces beyond possibility of being mended. This illustration alone is sufficient to establish the House of Israel and the House of Judah as two separate and distinct peoples. Judah has been, as illustrated in the broken bottle, a dispersed people and no longer a nation as a result of the fulfillment of the judgment pronounced upon them. For centuries Jerusalem was a desolate city in accordance with Jeremiah's prophecy:

"And I will make this city desolate, and an hissing; every one that passeth thereby shall be astonished and hiss because of all the plagues thereof." (Jer. 19:8.)

But the House of Israel was to turn from their evil ways and God's hand of final judgment was to be stayed. God is referring to the House of Israel when He says:

"At what instant I shall speak concerning a nation, and concerning a kingdom, to pluck up, and to pull down, and to destroy it: If that nation, against whom I have pronounced, turn from their evil, I will repent of the evil that I thought to do unto them." (Jer. 18:7-8.)

But the House of Judah, whom God had established

at Jerusalem with the Throne of David and the temple
in their midst, was warned:

"And at what instant I shall speak concerning a nation, and concerning a kingdom, to build and to plant
it; If it do evil in my sight, that it obey not my voice,
then I will repent of the good wherewith I said I would
benefit them." (Jer. 18: 9-10.)

This was the message Jeremiah was instructed to proclaim to Judah, warning that though they felt secure,
evil would come unless they repented and turned
wholeheartedly to the Lord. But they refused to heed
the prophet's warning. Just as surely as the descendants
of Judah are today a dispersed people in accordance
with the judgment passed upon them, without a government of their own and without a country, all in literal fulfillment of Jeremiah's prophecies, so the House
of Israel must be in the world today, a re-made vessel.
Judah was to be broken but the House of Israel was to
be refashioned as a potter would rework a clay vessel
which had been marred in fashioning upon his wheels.

THE PERFECT VESSEL

Jeremiah's prophecy of reshaping the clay of the
House of Israel throws a great deal of light on the
meaning of Paul's words when he quotes from Hosea,
who referred to the House of Israel, not Judah, when
he declared Israel was to become Lo-ammi, *i.e.*, not My
people. This is Paul's argument:

"Nay but, O man, who art thou that repliest against
God? Shall the thing formed say to him that formed

it, Why hast thou made me thus? Hath not the potter
power over the clay, of the same lump to make one
vessel unto honour [or distinction] and another unto
dishonour [or common use]? What if God, willing to
shew his wrath, and to make his power known, endured
with much longsuffering the vessels of wrath fitted to
destruction; And that he might make known the riches
of his glory on the vessels of mercy, which he had afore
prepared unto glory? Even us, whom he hath called,
not of the Jews only, but also of the Gentiles [marginal
rendering is: from among the nations]? As he saith also
in Osee [Hosea], I will call them my people, which
were not my people; and her beloved, which was not
beloved. And it shall come to pass that in the place
where it was said unto them, Ye are not my people;
there shall they be called the children of the living God.
Esaias [Isaiah] also crieth concerning Israel, Though
the number of the children of Israel be as the sand of
the sea, a remnant shall be saved. For he will finish the
work." (Romans 9: 20-28.)

Thus the House of Israel were to turn from their evil
ways and later appear, first apparently Gentiles, then
becoming a Christian people. They were to make their
calling and election sure by turning to the Lord, accepting Jesus Christ, whom the Jews rejected, and thus escape the type of judgment which finally overtook
Judah.

The "marred" House of Israel in the hands of the
Lord, like clay in the hand of the potter, has today
reappeared as the Anglo-Saxon-Celtic peoples who

alone meet the requirements as Israel because they have been reshaped and made over—a vessel unto mercy and honor—restored as a Christian people, sons of the living God. The day will come when castout Israel—the same clay God tried to fashion into a perfect kingdom prior to the great captivity under the Assyrians, but who were marred in the process—will stand forth before all people a perfect vessel in the sight of all. Israel is being fashioned by the Divine Potter now to perform a special task in His service. The completion of the vessel requires its firing in the tribulations and troubles which have come upon us as God's people as the age closes. We will come forth from the heat a perfect Kingdom ready to do His will and carry out His purposes.

Judah, however, having deserted God, lost the Kingdom (Matt. 21:43) and so the Lord through Jeremiah exclaimed:

"My people have abandoned Me for Delusions,—they offer incense, and stumble from their ancient pathways, to follow unpaved bye-paths." (Jer. 18:15 *F. F. Trans.*)

THE PLOT

Because of the severity of the judgment pronounced by Jeremiah, the people said:

"Come, and let us devise devices [plot] against Jeremiah; for the law shall not perish from the priest, nor counsel from the wise, nor the word from the prophet. Come, and let us smite him with the tongue, and let us not give heed to any of his words." (Jer. 18:18.)

One rendering defines "smitting with the tongue" to be "cut out his tongue." Of this we are certain that every device by which those who hated Jeremiah could slander him was tried in the hope of discouraging the prophet. He called upon God to remember their counsel against him and their plans to slay him. He asked God not to forgive their iniquities nor blot their sins out of His sight, but instead to deal with them in the time of His anger.

JEREMIAH IN THE STOCKS

When Pashur, the son of Immer, the priest, who was also Chief Governor in the House of the Lord, heard that Jeremiah prophesied such dire, irrevocable judgment for Judah and Jerusalem he arrested him and put the prophet in the stocks at the high gate of Benjamin, by the House of the Lord.

The stocks are an instrument of punishment used in comparatively modern times to confine the ankles of the prisoner. But the stocks used in Jeremiah's time kept the body in a bent position by confining the neck, arms and legs. This evidently was a climax in the suffering of the prophet and led him to curse the day of his birth, questioning if any good had come from the fact that it had been reported to his father that a son was born. For all he had seen all his life was labor, sorrow and days full of shame.

The next day Pashur took the prophet out of the stocks and Jeremiah said to him:

"The Lord hath not called thy name Pashur, but

Magor-missabib [*i.e.*, fear round about]. For thus saith the Lord, Behold, I will make thee a terror to thyself, and to all thy friends: and they shall fall by the sword of their enemies, and thine eyes shall behold it. . . . And thou, Pashur, and all that dwell in thine house shall go into captivity: and thou shalt come to Babylon, and there thou shalt die, and shalt be buried there, thou, and all thy friends, to whom thou hast prophesied lies." (Jer. 20: 3-6.)

THE BURNING WORDS

Jeremiah declared that God had enticed him into doing a work that caused him only trouble and persecution for he had become a daily reproach and derision. His experience in the stocks, with the suffering involved because of the message God had instructed him to give which stirred the people to the acts of violence against him, led him to exclaim:

"I will not make mention of him, nor speak any more in his name." (Jer. 20: 9.)

But Jeremiah could not keep from speaking for the zeal of the Lord was in his heart and he was compelled to fulfill the prophet's vow. So he said:

"But his word was in mine heart as a burning fire shut up in my bones, and I was weary with forebearing, and I could not stay." (Jer. 20: 9.)

In spite of the fact that every one was watching that they might keep each other informed concerning the prophet's movements and acts in the hope that he would leave an opening so that they might overpower him and take revenge, Jeremiah could not remain silent. In the difficult place in which he found himself he exclaimed:

"But the Lord is with me as a mighty terrible one; therefore my persecutors shall stumble, and they shall not prevail; they will be greatly ashamed; for they shall not prosper." (Jer. 20: 11.)

DESIRE FOR JUDGMENT

The human side is clearly depicted as Jeremiah, under suffering and persecution, desired to see those who were responsible for it all come to judgment:

"O Lord of hosts, that triest the righteous, and seest the reins and the heart, let me see thy vengeance on them: for unto thee have I opened my cause." (Jer. 20: 12.)

Over the years Jeremiah's attitude had been changing. At first he was definitely concerned for his people and would have willingly forgiven all their acts against him personally if only the coming evil might be averted. As time passed and he came to a fuller appreciation of their stubborn and evil ways he realized that there was no other course for God to follow except to carry out the verdict of judgment upon them. His own suffering, through persecution and misrepresentation, had clearly brought home to him this needed lesson.

THE BROKEN BOTTLE

Judah, the nation, likened to a fired bottle, was broken in pieces and could never again be restored to nationhood. Though the Zionists are today endeavoring to set up a Jewish state in Palestine, an abortive attempt to

restore the Kingdom of Judah, their efforts are doomed
to ultimate failure. There is not one shred of scriptural
justification whatever for their sponsored program for
an independent state in the endeavor to make Judah a
nation among the family of nations once more.

The present status of the Jew, a remnant of Judah,
is referred to by Jesus who said of the Jews for their
rejection of Him, "Behold, your house is left unto you
desolate" (Matt. 23: 38). This is confirmed in the fig
tree emblem (symbolical of the Jews) which Jesus
cursed for being unfruitful with the consequence that
it withered and died. When the Kingdom was taken
from the Jews for their unfruitfulness and given to a
nation which would bring forth the fruits thereof
(Matt. 21: 43) the end of the Jewish nation was at
hand. They withered and died to nationhood when the
Roman armies destroyed the city and Temple in 70 A.D.
The present hope of the Jews is not in their restoration
as a nation, for the broken bottle cannot be mended, but
in the individual acceptance of the Messiahship of Jesus
Christ that through Him each one may secure citizenship in His restored Kingdom.

CHAPTER VIII

THE MESSAGE TO THE HOUSE OF DAVID

Zedekiah, King of Judah, sent priests to Jeremiah asking him to inquire of the Lord concerning Nebuchadnezzar, King of Babylon, for he was making war against him. The King in his message to the prophet suggested that perhaps the Lord would work a miracle as He had often done and thereby force the King of Babylon to retreat.

This message came to Jeremiah just after his release from prison and at the very commencement of the war which was to end in the captivity of the House of Judah. The siege of Jerusalem had not yet begun but it was evident that the armies of Babylon were moving toward Palestine and Zedekiah was very much disturbed. His inquiry indicated that Jeremiah, though disliked and hated by many, was recognized as the prophet of the Lord. Also, the King was fully aware that God had delivered His people from disaster many times in the past and he hoped that He would do so again. Jeremiah's past warnings of coming disaster had not been taken seriously. The King, priests, princes and people had refused to turn from their evil ways and the trouble which he had predicted would come upon them from the north was now at hand—Nebuchadnezzar's armies were descending to besiege Jerusalem. The prophet's messages and warnings were being vindicated and the King requested Jeremiah to inquire of the Lord and secure His help in turning the armies of Babylon back. Jeremiah had pleaded and suffered at the hands of his people for nearly forty years and now that trouble was coming they turned to him to intercede with God in their behalf. Solomon's words of wisdom come to mind:

"But ye have set at nought all my counsel, and would none of my reproof. . . . . When your fear cometh as desolation, and your destruction cometh as a whirlwind; when distress and anguish come upon you. Then shall they call upon me, but I will not answer; they shall seek me early, but they shall not find me: For that they hated knowledge, and did not choose the fear of the Lord: They would none of my counsel: they despised all of my reproof. Therefore shall they eat of the fruit of their own way, and be filled with their own devices." (Prov. 1: 25-31.)

JEREMIAH'S REPLY

The end of the Kingdom of Judah was at hand and so Jeremiah replied to the King's message:

"Thus saith the Lord God of Israel; Behold, I will turn back the weapons of war that are in your hands, wherewith ye fight against the king of Babylon, and against the Chaldeans, which besiege you without the walls, and I will assemble them into the midst of this city." (Jer. 21: 4.)

Judah was to become impotent and her weapons useless, compelling her armies to retreat into the city. There the Lord declared:

"I myself will fight against you with outstretched

hand, and with a strong arm, even in anger, and in fury, and in great wrath. And I will smite the inhabitants of this city, both man and beast: they shall die of great pestilence." (Jer. 21: 5-6.)

Turning his attention to the House of David, Jeremiah continued with the message of the Lord:

"And afterward, saith the Lord, I will deliver Zedekiah king of Judah, and his servants, and the people and such as are left in this city from pestilence, from the sword, and from the famine, into the hand of Nebuchadnezzar king of Babylon, and into the hand of their enemies, and into the hand of those that seek their life: and he shall smite them with the edge of the sword; he shall not spare them, neither have pity, nor have mercy." (Jer. 21: 7.)

THE PROPHET'S COUNSEL

As will be shown later, Zedekiah was carried away into Babylon where he died. Jeremiah was then instructed to tell the people that God had set two ways before them:

"Thus saith the Lord; Behold, I set before you the way of life, and the way of death. He that abideth in this city shall die by the sword, and by the famine, and by the pestilence: but he that goeth out, and falleth to the Chaldeans that besiege you, he shall live, and his life shall be unto him a prey. For I have set my face against this city for evil, and not for good, saith the Lord: it shall be given into the hand of the king of

Babylon, and he shall burn it with fire." (Jer. 21: 8-10.)

Thus Jeremiah counseled the people to surrender to the King of Babylon, and in so doing save their lives, for the city would be destroyed. The prophet called upon the House of David to keep judgment and do righteously and deliver men from oppression. The administration of the law was stressed that no wrong be done to the stranger, the fatherless or the widow and that innocent blood be not shed. This message was not only addressed to the King of Judah who was sitting upon the Throne of David in the time of Jeremiah, but it had a far wider application. It was an admonition to the House of David throughout the ages to recognize the law and the need of keeping judgment in righteousness wherever that House ruled over His people.

REASON FOR JUDGMENT

Judgment had overtaken Jerusalem and Judea as well as the House of David because of oppression and violence and Jeremiah prophesied as one consequence of the coming destruction of the city:

"And many nations shall pass by this city, and they shall say every man to his neighbour, Wherefore hath the Lord done thus unto this great city? Then they shall answer, Because they have forsaken the covenant of the Lord their God, and worshipped other gods, and served them." (Jer. 22: 8-9.)

This prophecy was literally fulfilled for down the ages the continued desolation of Jerusalem has been recognized as the result of both Israel and Judah having forsaken the Covenant when they turned away from God to worship idols. Neither atheists nor agnostics can deny this fact; one among many others which substantiates the truth of Scripture by the fulfillment of the prophetic predictions of its prophets.

Let us pause here and review the contemporary history of those times and the events which ultimately led to the desolation of Jerusalem and sent the House of Judah into captivity. These historical facts are taken from the Bible, from Josephus and from the outline of those historical events as given by Professor C. A. L. Totten.

Jeremiah was born during the 40th year of Manasseh's reign. Intoxicated by power and poisoned by Phoenician and Babylonian flattery and idolatry, the early manhood of Manasseh was stained by cruelty of the worst kind, during which prophets (among them Isaiah) and saintly men and women were massacred. His first twenty-one years of misrule were followed by his sudden conversion while temporarily a prisoner of war. Following his release he instituted a final thirty-four years of wise and pious government, but of them we have little record.

BIRTH OF JEREMIAH

Nearly nineteen of those quiet years had already passed when Jeremiah was born. Many of the prophet's near relatives were not only in the service of the King but were allied by blood and marriage to the royal family. Among these we find Shallum, the uncle of Jeremiah, whose son, Hanameel, was about the prophet's age. Ahikam, who afterwards became prime minister, was also a relative and a great champion of Jeremiah and his family. Neriah, another relative, must have been somewhat older, as his sons Baruch and Seraiah later became pupils of Jeremiah.

According to a Rabbinical tradition quoted by Plumtre, the whole of this family circle, including the most prominent courtiers of Josiah, were lineally descended from Rahab (Joshua 6: 17), and were therefore closely related to the princes of the House of David.

There is every reason to believe that Hilkiah, who was Josiah's High Priest, and Jeremiah of Libnah, are identical with Hilkiah, the Priest, and Jeremiah of Anathoth. Both Libnah and Anathoth (1 Chron. 6: 57-60) are listed among the thirteen cities assigned to Eleazer's house of Priests and Levites, and Shallum, the father of Hilkiah, appears to have inherited property in each locality. For awhile Hilkiah dwelt at Anathoth where lay the paternal inheritance but, upon the death of his father, Shallum, he seems to have moved to Libnah, relinquishing Anathoth to his elder brother Shallum.

This was evidently after Jeremiah's birth, which occurred at Anathoth during the elder Shallum's High Priesthood, and while Hilkiah himself was only an ordinary priest. It seems to have antedated Jeremiah's marriage and the birth of his daughter Hamutal (II

Kings 23: 31) who eventually became the second wife and Queen consort of Josiah.

Many years later, and for lack of heirs, Hanameel, the son of Shallum, Jeremiah's uncle, offered Anathoth to the prophet. Jeremiah purchased it and became the owner of both properties in his own right (Jer. 32: 7).

Jeremiah married a Levite maiden of Libnah, the city to which his parents had moved upon the death of Shallum, and he became the father of Hamutal. This daughter seems to have been the prophet's only child; at least she is the only one of whom we have any record.

Manasseh died when Jeremiah was fifteen years old and Ammon, the father of Josiah, came to the throne. He ruled for a very brief period and the young king's excesses duplicated the worst days of Manasseh. Because of his unreasonable cruelty, he was killed by his own servants.

Josiah ascended the throne at the age of eight and under wise tutors he was carefully trained in the path of virtue and righteousness. At the age of thirteen he married Zebudah, the daughter of Pedaiah of Rumah. She gave birth to a son, the unfortunate Jehoiakim (II Kings 23:36).

Following Josiah's second marriage, when Hamutal became his wife, the King began his reformation, purging Jerusalem of the high places and groves and destroying the idolatrous images (II Chron. 34: 3-7).

BOOK OF THE LAW DISCOVERED

Jeremiah was commissioned in the thirteenth year of Josiah's reign (3377 A.M., or 619 B.C.). This same year Nabopolassar, father of Nebuchadnezzar, revolted from Assyria and ascended the throne of Babylon. Five years later Hilkiah discovered a cabinet among the treasure chests in the Temple as Josiah was carrying on the good work of restoring the House of God in Jerusalem. When this chest was opened it was found to contain a complete copy of the law, with the five books of Moses, the only copy that had escaped destruction. This was passed on to the King who gathered his cabinet together and made inquiry of the Lord concerning the fate of the nation. The Prophetess Huldah foretold the approaching downfall of the nation, but assured the king it would not occur in his reign.

A solemn assembly was called of the people and the words of the law were read. The King renewed his oath upon the ancient Coronation Stone of Bethel* (II Chron. 34: 29-33; II Kings 23: 1-3), *as the manner was* in the coronation of Joash and all his fathers. Among those who came to this assembly was Jeremiah, who evidently listened with a great heart hunger, greedily devouring every word. Speaking afterward to the Lord of this meeting he exclaimed:

"Thy words were found, and I did eat them, and thy word was unto me the joy and rejoicing of mine heart; for I am called by thy name, O Lord God of Hosts." (Jer. 15: 16.)

* See "The Stone of History," DESTINY for July, 1944.

RESTORATION OF WORSHIP

This great discovery was followed by the crowning act of the restoration of the worship of God, the calling of the people to one of the most famous Passovers ever celebrated (II Chron. 35: 1-19). Josiah spared no effort to make his work of restoration complete. He even employed detectives to ferret out all who worked any abominations in the land of Judah (II Kings 23: 24) and succeeded in putting down all open opposition to Jehovah, the God of Israel.

Hamutal, his second wife, gave birth to two sons, Jehoahaz (II Kings 23: 31) and the famous Zedekiah, who became the last monarch of the line of David to rule in Jerusalem. A few years later Jehoiachin, probably the only son of Jehoiakim, was born and thus the *legal* claim to the sceptre remaining in the hand of Zeludah's branch of Josiah's family seemed to be assured.

During the quiet years following Zedekiah's birth Palestine seemed to have fully recovered her vitality and strength but, after all, the reformation was only an enforced one. The sins of Judah broke out afresh as soon as the personal influence of Josiah was withdrawn. The fierceness of God's anger continued unappeased because of the hidden sins in secret places to which Jeremiah alludes again and again.

The penalty for the sins of Manasseh and his contemporaries obeyed a universal law, and in due time was literally "visited upon the third and fourth generation"

—upon Jehoiakim and Jehoiachin his son, and upon Zedekiah and his sons.

UNHOLY ALLIANCE

The reign of Josiah had attained a measure of normalcy and would have continued longer in such a course had he not made a fatal mistake in policy. It was in the latter part of his thirty-first year as King that Pharaoh-nechoh came up against the King of Babylon, with whom Josiah formed an offensive and defensive alliance. In spite of Pharaoh's disavowal of any hostile intent against Judah, Josiah espoused the side of Nabopolassar, the new King of Assyria. Probably one of the causes of this alliance was the unwarranted invasion of neutral territory by the Egyptians whose armies skirted the western borders of Palestine. Josiah's army shared in his resentment and so the King went out to meet the Egyptians at Megiddo with the intention of cutting off their retreat but unwisely failed to wait for a junction with the troops of Babylon.

It was a short and decisive battle wherein Josiah was fatally wounded and died in his chariot on the return to Jerusalem. All Jerusalem mourned because of his sudden death while it is recorded that Jeremiah lamented for Josiah, his own son-in-law (II Chron. 35:25).

In the confusion incident upon Josiah's sudden death Jeremiah might have influenced the people to place Jehoahaz, Josiah's eldest son by Hamutal, upon the throne instead of his half-brother Eliakim. Jehoahaz was not worthy, however, for he did evil in the sight of the Lord. His downfall was no doubt brought about by the faction opposed to him and in favor of Eliakim, who turned to Egypt for assistance.

PHARAOH TAKES JERUSALEM

Pharaoh-nechoh, diverted from his original intention of seeking battle with the Babylonians, turned aside to besiege Jerusalem. The city fell without resistance and Jehoahaz surrendered to Pharaoh. Nechoh thereupon made Eliakim, the son of Queen Zebudah, King of Judah instead of his half-brother and changed his name to Jehoiakim. He laid a heavy tribute upon the land and departed for Egypt carrying Jehoahaz with him as a captive. It appears that Jehoahaz died in Egypt without any posterity while Jehoiakim ruled for the next three years, sending annual tribute to Pharaoh-nechoh. Queen Hamutal withdrew from public life, returning to Libnah where she seems to have devoted her attention to Mattaniah (Zedekiah) her son. Jeremiah spent most of his time in Jerusalem where his labors as a prophet were daily increasing in magnitude. It appears that Jeremiah's own wife had died and he was contemplating a second marriage with some one in Jerusalem which God forbade (Jer. 16: 1-2).

The Egyptian king returned to the land of Judah no more for the Babylonian Empire had reached its full development and Nebuchadnezzar, the son of Nabopolassar, having destroyed Nechoh and his power at Carchemish, invaded Palestine with a powerful army, and at last acquired all of the territory that by previous conquest had belonged to Pharaoh-nechoh, "even from the river of Egypt to the river Euphrates" (II Kings 24: 7).

DANIEL TAKEN TO BABYLON

Nebuchadnezzar next directed his attention to the troublesome city of Jerusalem and soon brought it into subjection. Jehoiakim was at this time bound in chains and was at the point of being carried away to Babylon when he purchased his release with money and a promise to pay yearly tribute to Babylon. Nebuchadnezzar accepted his promises and carried away to Babylon part of the vessels in the House of the Lord and some of the King's sons and of the princes of the land, who according to previous prophecy (Isa. 39: 7) became eunuchs in his palace. Among these were Daniel and his companions.

Jehoiakim for the next three years faithfully paid tribute to Nebuchadnezzar but, upon hearing that the King of Babylon had made an expedition against the Egyptians, he rebelled against him. During the next four years Babylon was too much occupied in other localities to bother with Judah but finally Nebuchadnezzar returned to Palestine and Josephus tells us:

"Slew such as were in the flower of their age, and such as were of the greatest dignity, together with their king Jehoiakim, whom he commanded to be thrown before the walls without burial."

A single son of Jehoiakim remained, Jehoiachin, whom Nebuchadnezzar, prior to his departure, placed upon his father's throne. Taking three thousand of the surviving principal persons, among whom was the prophet Ezekiel, he set out for home, but before leaving Palestine he repented of his selection. Josephus says:

"But a terror seized on the king of Babylon who had given the kingdom to Jehoiachin, and that immediately, for he was afraid that he would bear him a grudge, because he slew his father, and thereupon should make the country rebel."

JEHOIACHIN TAKEN TO BABYLON

Therefore, Jehoiachin, also known as Jeconiah and Coniah, reigned but three months and ten days when another Babylonian army under Nebuzaradan as Captain of the hosts returned to Jerusalem, recaptured it and, continuing his devastations, carried away the King and his house, ten thousand captives and all the craftmen and smiths, none left behind but the poorest of the people (II Kings 24: 8-14.)

ZEDEKIAH MADE KING

But Jerusalem still had eleven more years of grace. Thus it happened that before Nebuzaradan left for Babylon with his spoils and captives, Nebuchadnezzar joined him in Palestine and sent to Libnah for Hamutal and her son. He then made Mattaniah, the last remaining son of Josiah and the uncle of Jehoiachin (Coniah), the tributary king of Judah and changed his name to Zedekiah. According to Josephus, Nebuchadnezzar:

"Made him take an oath that he would certainly keep

the kingdom for him, and make no innovation, nor have any league of friendship with the Egyptians."

This brief outline of the history of events brings us to the end of Jehoiachin's rule and the elevation of Zedekiah to the throne of David. Jeremiah foretold the judgments to come upon the kings of Judah. Of Jehoahaz he says:

"For thus saith the Lord touching Shallum [Jehoahaz] the son of Josiah king of Judah, which reigned instead of Josiah his father, which went forth out of this place [Pharaoh-nechoh had carried him away to Egypt], he shall not return thither anymore! But he shall die in the place whither they have led him captive, and shall see this land no more." (Jer. 22: 11-12.)

WOE FOR UNRIGHTEOUSNESS

Jehoahaz never returned to Palestine and died in Egypt.

Jeremiah pronounced woe upon those who build in unrighteousness and use their neighbour's services without giving wages for work done. Pointing his finger at Jehoiakim as one guilty of injustice and of shedding innocent blood, Jeremiah declared:

"Therefore thus saith the Lord concerning Jehoiakim the son of Josiah king of Judah; They shall not lament for him, saying, Ah my brother! or, Ah sister! they shall not lament for him saying, Ah Lord! or, Ah his glory! He shall be buried with the burial of an ass, drawn and cast forth beyond the gates of Jerusalem." (Jer. 22: 18-19.)

This curse was fulfilled when Nebuchadnezzar ordered Jehoiakim's body thrown before the walls of Jerusalem without burial.

The judgments pronounced against Jerusalem for her evil came upon the city as history shows and the nobles and princes and many of the people were carried away to Babylon before the final desolation that ended in the destruction of the city itself. Jeremiah turned to declare certain things concerning Coniah, or Jehoiachin, the son of Jehoiakim:

"As I live, saith the Lord, though Coniah the son of Jehoiakim king of Judah were the signet upon my right hand, yet would I pluck thee thence; And I will give thee into the hand of them that seek thy life, and into the hand of them whose face thou fearest, even into the hand of Nebuchadnezzar king of Babylon, and into the hand of the Chaldeans. And I will cast thee out, and thy mother that bare thee [II Kings 24: 15], into another country, where ye were not born; and there shall ye die. But to the land whereunto they desire to return, thither shall they not return." (Jer. 22: 24-27.)

This is exactly what came to pass and Nebuchadnezzar did carry Coniah (Jehoiachin) with his mother and family to Babylon. None of them returned from the land of their captors to Palestine again.

THE SIGNET RING

Now a signet ring upon the right hand, bearing the name or seal of its owner, when given into the care of another, has as its objective the accomplishment of a definite and extremely important purpose. The removal of Coniah to another land with his family was as essential to God's plans in preserving the line of our Lord as the removal of Joseph to Egypt was essential for the preservation of his father's household. Through Jeremiah God declares that the accomplishment of His plans is so important that if Coniah were His signet ring he would still be given to Nebuchadnezzar and taken to Babylon.

IMPORTANT QUESTIONS

The entire thinking of the ecclesiastical schools and the literature written about Coniah needs drastic revision because of the absolute failure to recognize the important part this man of the royal line of David was destined to play. Coniah has been woefully maligned as an evil man who suffered a fate comparable to his wickedness when actually God removed him from Palestine to protect and preserve the family line of our Lord.

Jeremiah continues:

"Is this man Coniah a despised broken idol? is he a vessel wherein is no pleasure? wherefore are they cast out, he and his seed, and are cast into a land which they know not?" (Jer. 22: 28.)

These are very pertinent questions and are being asked for a particular reason. The very fact that Jeremiah raised the issues involved in these questions should put the reader immediately on guard that Coniah's immediate family was not the hopeless and despised line that Bible scholars and students have assumed.

Ferrar Fenton translates:

"Is this man Koniah a contemptible broken pot? or a thing in which there is no use? Why do they throw him, and his race away, and fling to a land which they know not?"

The answer is no. He and his line were not contemptible, nor a part of the broken pot or vessel to which Jeremiah had likened Judah which had become unusable. God was to use Coniah and his descendants and there was a definite plan to this end which was aided by his being carried away to Babylon. There he and his house were preserved and his seed kept from disaster and destruction so that at the end of seventy years of captivity they might return to Palestine. For it was of that branch of the Royal House of David that our Lord came!

ELEVATION OF JEHOIACHIN

Further light is shed on Jehoiachin's (Coniah's) state in the land of his captors in the following:

"And it came to pass in the seven and thirtieth year of the captivity of Jehoiachin king of Judah, in the twelfth month, in the five and twentieth day of the month, that Evil-merodach king of Babylon in the first year of his reign lifted up the head of Jehoiachin king of Judah, and brought him forth out of prison. And spake kindly unto him, and set his throne above the throne of the kings that were with him in Babylon, And changed his prison garments: and he did continually eat bread before him all the days of his life. And for his diet, there was a continual diet given him of the king of Babylon, every day a portion until the day of his death, all the days of his life." (Jer. 52: 31-34.)

Why is this account of Jehoiachin's good treatment given? The answers to the questions propounded by Jeremiah give the reason and, because the statement following these questions has been completely misunderstood, men have jumped to the conclusion that because God ordered Jeremiah to pronounce Coniah childless, insofar as a succession of rulers upon the throne of David ruling over Judah was concerned, that God had rejected him and his seed altogether. Jeremiah said:

"O earth, earth, earth, hear the word of the Lord. Thus saith the Lord, Write ye this man childless, a man that shall not prosper in his days: for no man of his seed shall prosper, sitting upon the throne of David, and ruling any more in Judah." (Jer. 22: 29-30.)

RULING OVER JUDAH

The fact that Coniah would not prosper in his day and no man of his seed would rule any more in Judah is in itself evidence that he was not literally childless. The record states otherwise (I Chron. 3: 17-18) for he had seven sons. However, insofar as a successor on the throne of David ruling over Judah was concerned, he was, for the record, childless.

In the line of our Lord, Matthew mentions Jechonias (Coniah) and his son Salathiel, and those who reason that, because of Jeremiah's statement, Coniah could not possibly be an ancestor of our Lord forget that the curse of childlessness applied only to "sitting upon the throne of David *and ruling any more in Judah.*"*

The Jews themselves refused to allow Jesus to rule over them and when He referred to their attitude, He mentioned those citizens who hated Him and who were declaring, "We will not have this man to reign over us" (Luke 19: 14).

No man of the line of Coniah was acceptable to the Jews, not even Jesus Christ, and so they rejected Him. When He returns to take over the reins of government He will receive *as a gift,* not by right of descent from the reigning line, the throne of His father David:

"And the Lord God shall give unto him the throne of his father David: And he shall reign over the house of Jacob [not Judah] for ever; and of his kingdom there shall be no end." (Luke 1: 32-33.)

From the time of Coniah to the present day there has been no man of the line of David ruling on a throne over the House of Judah. The nearest they came to receiving a king was the occasion when Jesus presented Himself to the nation of the Jews, but they refused to accept Him as their King.

By a careful analysis of Jeremiah's statements we discover, then, that Coniah and his family were not the despised and rejected branch of David's line as has been so universally taught. He was taken from prison and later in Babylon was well treated, being protected from the ravages of war which enveloped Palestine and de-

* See Appendix, "Which Genealogy?"

stroyed all the males of the seed royal when King Zedekiah's sons were slain and he was taken captive. How
the reigning line of the House of David was preserved
after the death of Zedekiah in Babylon is still another
chapter in this fascinating story.

CHAPTER IX

THE BASKETS OF GOOD AND BAD FIGS

Having finished his prophecy concerning Coniah, Jeremiah turned once again to the ecclesiastical and civil leaders of his people and warned that as rulers and instructors their responsibility was great in that they had failed in guiding the people in the ways of righteousness. They were accused of failing to visit the people with that care and love which are the attributes of a good pastor, nor had they given wise and godly instruction as true teachers in Israel. As a result violence and discord marred their rule. Jeremiah looked forward to a day to come when, following the deportation, captivity and scattering of Israel and Judah, God declared:

"I will gather the remnant of my flock out of all countries whither I have driven them, and will bring them again to their folds [homes]; and they shall be fruitful and increase." (Jer. 23: 3.)

FOOLISH LEADERS

Because the leaders of His people neglected their duty and were guilty of misrule in the Kingdom, God declared He would take good care to see that they were punished for the evil they committed. Men aspire to occupy places of authority over God's people; yet many fail to recognize the tremendous responsibility such authority places upon them, nor are they aware that God will require an accounting of their stewardship as a leader among His people. Not only did Jeremiah condemn the irresponsible leadership of his day, but the burden of his message, and that of other prophets concerning foolish leaders, is a condemnation of those men who misrule His people throughout the centuries. The Lord states a day is coming when:

"I will set up shepherds over them which shall feed them; and they shall fear no more, nor be dismayed, neither shall they be lacking, saith the Lord." (Jer. 23: 4.)

THE COMING BRANCH

As a result of this statement, the prophecy follows of the coming of the Messiah, Jesus Christ:

"Behold, the days come, saith the Lord, that I will raise unto David a righteous Branch, and a King shall reign and prosper, and shall execute judgment and justice in the earth." (Jer. 23: 5.)

The Hebrew word translated *branch* in this verse is *tsemach* and means a sprout from the root, not from the branch of the tree, and specifically refers to the Messiah as the coming King who will rule in righteousness. The name of the brightest star in the Zodiac sign of Virgo is *Zemach* in Hebrew and means branch. The following data concerning Virgo is quoted from *The Stars Declare God's Handiwork.**

"Virgo (the virgin)—Virgo lies about half north and half south of the equator and south of Coma and Boötes. It is one of the larger constellations. The sun occupies

* 50 cents, postpaid, DESTINY PUBLISHERS, Merrimac, Mass.

Virgo for forty-three days, passing through it from September 14th to October 29th. Most of its stars being comparatively faint and much scattered, it is difficult to trace. The pagans considered it a goddess with wings, bearing a sheaf of wheat in one hand. The outline of the maiden is so entirely imaginary it is almost impossible for the observer to follow it, but the Virgin, or the promised seed of the woman, is the theme of this constellation.

"Stripped of idolatry and paganism, Virgo represents a woman with a branch in her right hand, and some ears of corn in her left. The meaning of the Hebrew name for this sign is *a virgin* while the meaning in Arabic is *a branch*. Thus is pictured the fulfillment of Isaiah 7: 14 as quoted by Matthew, 'Behold, a virgin shall be with child, and bring forth a son, and they shall call his name Emmanuel, which being interpreted is, God with us.' (Matt. 1: 23.)

"The bright star in the ear of corn in her hand is called in Arabic AL ZIMACH, which means the branch. So Zechariah writes of this branch to come when he says, 'For, behold, I will bring forth my servant the Branch.' (Zech. 3: 8.)

"One of the stars in the arm carrying the branch is called AL MUREDDIN, which means *who shall come down or who shall have dominion*. Psalms 72: 8 states, 'He shall have dominion also from sea to sea.' This star is also known as VINDEMIATRIX, a Chaldee word which means *the son*, or *branch*, who *cometh*."

Jeremiah thus prophesies of the coming of *The*

Branch who as the coming King will establish righteousness and rule with judgment and justice and so the prophet continues:

"In his days Judah shall be saved, and Israel shall dwell safely: and this is His name whereby he shall be called, THE LORD OUR RIGHTEOUSNESS (*i.e., Jehovah Zidkenu*)." (Jer. 23: 6.)

ISRAEL'S DELIVERANCE

In that day Jeremiah declares it will no more be said:

"The Lord liveth, which brought up the children of Israel out of the land of Egypt; But, the Lord liveth, which brought up and which led the seed of the house of Israel out of the north country, and from all countries whither I had driven them; and they shall dwell in their own land." (Jer. 23: 7-8,)

For centuries the Christian Church has failed to recognize that the House of Israel is separate and distinct from Judah but a day is coming when all Israel, and the Church, will awaken to the full realization of the identity of God's people in the world today. Ezekiel declares:

"So the house of Israel shall know that I am the Lord their God from that day and forward. . . . Then shall they know that I am the Lord their God, which caused them to be led into captivity among the heathen: but I have gathered them unto their own land, and have left none of them any more there. Neither will I hide my face any more from them: for I have poured out

my spirit upon the house of Israel saith the Lord God."
(Ez. 39: 22-29.)

When the House of Israel is finally revealed to all
the world as the nation and company of nations of
prophecy, the ancient deliverance from the bondage of
Egypt will sink into insignificance in comparison to the
greater deliverance of the people from the bondage of
modern misrule and economic oppression as the judgments of God destroy the entire system of Mammon.

HISTORY PREWRITTEN

The House of Israel was carried away into Assyrian
captivity and disappeared from the land of their captors
into the countries north of Palestine. In the centuries
which passed after their disappearance this people,
under different names, moved west through southern
and central Europe to the appointed place, the isles
north and west of Palestine. God gathered His people
into a land of their own and to the inheritance of the
"desolate heritages" of prophecy as they spread out
from their island kingdom to the North American continent, to Australia, New Zealand and other places. The
marvelous providence of God will be made known to
all men when the facts of history are fully revealed,
confirming prophecy as history prewritten.

DESPAIR OVER FALSE PROPHETS

Jeremiah deplored the utterances and acts of the false
prophets. The depraved conditions extending into the
House of the Lord caused him to declare his heart was

broken because of the evil doings of those men. The description of the conditions of the prophet's time could as readily apply to conditions in our own land today. Instead of preaching the truth the prophets and priests were leading the people astray by presenting false and evil doctrines. All this evil is being duplicated in this twentieth century in the evil doctrines of the higher critic and modernist whose false teachings are leading the people away from truth as they turn away from belief in the accuracy of God's Word written. The modernist schools of thought belittle the inspiration of the Scriptures and as a result thousands have turned away from reliance upon the authority of the Bible.

MODERNIST TEACHINGS

The present day miracle-denying, Christ-belittling teachings of modernism are but a counterpart of the false doctrines of the prophets and teachers of Jeremiah's time. The prophet declared they were active in the House of the Lord and we find today many of the pulpits in our land occupied by such wolves in sheep's clothing—atheists, garbed in the mantle of the clergy, presenting the worldly wisdom of the unregenerated to their congregations. As in Jeremiah's time, so now:

"The land is full of adulterers; for because of swearing the land mourneth; the pleasant places of the wilderness are dried up, and their course [violence] is evil, and their force [or energy] is not right." (Jer. 23: 10.)

Jeremiah pointed out there would be only one end

for the evil course the priests and prophets had chosen. Their very acts, he declared, strengthened the hands of evil-doers, just as the false doctrines of modernists today turn men from the way of life and salvation in Jesus Christ and harden them in their unbelief. Then, as now, the false leaders did not turn from their wickedness, nor were they afraid as they led the people astray. The judgments pronounced upon the false prophets of Jeremiah's time are also a condemnation and judgment upon the false leaders of our day:

"Therefore thus saith the Lord of hosts concerning the prophets; Behold, I will feed them with wormwood, and make them drink the water of gall: for from the prophets of Jerusalem is profaneness [hypocrisy] gone forth into all the land." (Jer. 23: 15.)

Ferrar Fenton translates this:

"The Lord of Hosts consequently says this against those preachers, 'I will consume them with suffering, and give them opiates to drink,—for corruption comes to all the country from the preachers of Jerusalem.'"

The fact that the Lord declares He will give these preachers opiates, *i.e.*, put them to sleep, accounts for their total lack of understanding the Bible and the words of the prophets even when events become so evident that the simple can see and recognize their meaning.

RESULT OF FALSE DOCTRINES

These are the conditions extant today as a result of the false doctrines and teachings which have brought spiritual corruption to our land. Unbelief in the Word of God is now widespread and the dissemination of poisonous doctrines from our seminaries and colleges has spread into every city, town and hamlet, polluting the wells of spiritual understanding. The evils which Jeremiah complained had in his day corrupted the land are rampant today and so the word of the Lord spoken by Jeremiah is germane in this generation:

"Listen not to the messages of the Preachers who preach to you. They preach nonsense to you,— a vision from their own hearts." (Jer. 23: 16, *F. F. Trans.*)

NOT OF THE LORD

The words they speak are not from the Lord. This injunction of the Lord is being literally fulfilled today for many are refusing to listen to the doctrines of modernism. Church attendance continues to drop and weekly prayer meetings and evening services cease through lack of support. Many who do attend services pay little attention to what is being said from the pulpit for the words of the preachers are meaningless and without Spirit when they deny the truth of God's Word.

The preachers of Jeremiah's time were assuring the people of peace in spite of the warnings given by Jeremiah of the certainty of coming disaster. The prophets also were trying to comfort the people by proclaiming no harm would come to them, for it was more profitable to them to preach what the people preferred to hear. This same attitude is being taken by those who today refuse to preach the word of the Lord, for modern preachers can be asked the identical question Jeremiah put to the false preachers of his time:

"For who hath stood in the counsel of the Lord, and hath perceived and heard his word? who has marked his word and heard it?" (Jer. 23: 18.)

LEADERS REPUDIATED

The Spirit of the Lord did not move the false preachers and teachers to utter the nonsense they preached for they did not stand in the secret counsels of the Lord; rather they spoke from their own hearts. The Lord repudiated them all, declaring He had not sent them, for if they had been in His counsel they would have taught the people to hear and believe His word and they themselves would have turned from their evil ways.

GOD KNOWS ALL

God challenged them by asking if He is so circumscribed that He is unaware of what is going on everywhere?

"Can any hide himself in secret places that I shall not see him? saith the Lord. Do not I fill heaven and earth? saith the Lord." (Jer. 23: 24.)

The Lord declares He has heard all the evil and lies the false teachers have been practicing out of the deceit of their own hearts, causing His people to forget Him. Their concepts and worldly wisdom He calls as worthless as an ordinary dream. Their program should not be dignified by suggesting they had received an inspired vision from Him. They are given His condemnation:

"The prophet that hath a dream, let him tell a dream; and he that hath my word, let him speak my word faithfully. What is the chaff to the wheat? saith the Lord." (Jer. 23: 28.)

There is no nourishment in chaff and in like manner the doctrines of modernism completely lack the life-giving qualities of the Spirit so necessary to strengthen God's people. What the people need today is spiritual fortitude to meet the conditions of trouble and distress around us. God likens His Word to a fire that consumes and a hammer that can break the hardest rock into pieces. The preachers who were speaking words out of their own hearts were failing to use the strengthening Word of the Lord to overcome evil and break down the opposition of evil doers. As judgment came upon the generation of Jeremiah's time, so will it come upon every generation that turns against God and His word.

Of Judah and Jerusalem the Lord declared:

"And I will bring an everlasting reproach upon you, and a perpetual shame, which shall not be forgotten." (Jer. 23: 40.)

History has amply verified the accuracy of the fulfillment of this prophecy in the destruction of Jerusalem and the deportation of its inhabitants to Babylon. A period of partial desolation followed the early deportation of the House of Judah and the desolation became final as the result of the destruction of the city by the Romans in 70 A.D. For years Judea was a deserted land and Jerusalem a city forsaken.

THE BASKETS OF FIGS

In order to illustrate the difference between the two groups of captives, God gave Jeremiah a vision of two baskets of figs. The prophet declares:

"The Lord showed me, and, behold, two baskets of figs were set before the temple of the Lord, after that Nebuchadnezzar king of Babylon had carried away captive Jeconiah the son of Jehoiakim king of Judah, and the princes of Judah, with the carpenters and smiths, from Jerusalem, and had brought them to Babylon. One basket had very good figs, even like the figs that are first ripe: and the other basket had very naughty figs, which could not be eaten, they were so bad." (Jer. 24: 1-2.)

When asked what he saw Jeremiah described the two baskets of figs and then the word of the Lord came to him saying:

"Thus saith the Lord, the God of Israel, Like these good figs, so will I acknowledge them that are carried away captive of Judah, whom I have sent out of this place into the land of the Chaldeans for their good. For I will set mine eyes upon them for good, and I will bring them again to this land: and I will build them, and not pull them down; and I will plant them and not pluck them up. And I will give them an heart to know me, that I am the Lord; and they shall be my people, and I will be their God; for they shall return unto me with their whole heart." (Jer. 24: 5-7.)

THE GOOD FIGS

Who had been carried away to Babylon at this time, of whom the Lord was speaking? Daniel and his companions were in that group but as these men were made eunuchs by the King of Babylon, and would therefore have no posterity, the prophecy could not apply to descendants of theirs. Contrary to present accepted teaching concerning Coniah, and according to the facts presented in the previous chapter, Coniah, or Jeconiah, also called Jehoiachin, with his descendants, were part of the basket of good figs. Also numbered among the good figs were those of Judah whose descendants are not known or recognized in the world today as Jews but whose forefathers left the land of their Babylonian captors and became the progenitors of the Jutlanders, Scots, etc. Many among these people became Christianized and thus were numbered, in accordance with Jeremiah's prophecy, among His people who accepted the Lord as their God.

CONIAH AND FAMILY

As previously pointed out, Coniah and his family were removed to Babylon for their own good. This is exactly what Jeremiah was told was the purpose of the early deportation to Babylon of those of the captivity who were taken to the land of the Chaldeans prior to the destruction of Jerusalem and the beginning of the final captivity of Judah.

Coniah's descendants returned to Palestine at the end of the seventy years of Babylonian captivity. It was from this branch of the House of David that our Lord came and in acknowledging His Son Jesus Christ God certainly elevated Coniah's house to a place of pre-eminence. The prophecy that no man of this line would prosper upon the throne of David ruling any more in Judah was literally fulfilled and in conformity with this statement Jesus Christ Himself was rejected as King by the Jews. The disciples of our Lord and the early members of the Christian Church constituted the nucleus of a chosen group who were given a heart to know God, for with the first Pentecost after our Lord's resurrection there was laid a foundation of righteousness in Israel through which those in Israel who would believe could be recovenanted to God.

THE EVIL FIGS

The basket of evil figs which were so bad they couldn't be eaten represented Zedekiah, King of Judah, and his princes. It will be seen later on in the story that there was a discrimination among the members of Zedekiah's family; not all of them went into the basket of bad figs and came under the subsequent curse. A selection from among them was made when the King's daughters were set apart to continue the reigning line of kings upon the throne of David. Among the people whom Nebuchadnezzar left in the land were those numbered with the bad figs, together with the colony which had fled to Egypt to escape the King of Babylon and were dwelling there. Of them the Lord said:

"And I will deliver them to be removed into all the

kingdoms of the earth for their hurt, to be a reproach and a proverb, a taunt and a curse, in all places whither I shall drive them. And I will send the sword, the famine, and the pestilence, among them, till they be consumed from off the land that I gave unto them and to their fathers." (Jer. 24: 9-10.)

Ferrar Fenton translates the passage that God will make them:

"A seed of evil to all the kingdoms of the earth, as a reproach and a proverb; to be a slander, and a curse, in every place to which I drive them. I will also send sword, famine, and plague to harass them from off the land which I gave to them and to their forefathers."

Moffatt translates:

"I will make them an object of disgust to every kingdom in the world, a derision, a byword, a taunt, and a curse, wherever I drive them; also, I will send the sword, famine, and pestilence among them, till they are consumed out of the land that I gave to them and to their fathers."

The Douay Version of the Bible states that they were to be delivered up to vexation and affliction while the American Standard Bible declares they were to be tossed to and fro among all the kingdoms of the earth for evil.

It is certain that a remnant of the survivors of both groups of those carried away captive to Babylon returned to Judea and Jerusalem at the end of the 70 years. Some of that remnant were to be blessed. The family of Coniah of the House of David was so blessed in the birth of the Messiah, Jesus Christ. A remnant from the tribe of Benjamin also returned and became the Galileans who constituted most of the followers of Jesus Christ who accepted Christianity in the first century. But there also returned a remnant of those taken captive with Zedekiah whose descendants were the Jews of our Lord's day. Here are the bad figs of whom Jesus said:

"If God were your Father, ye would love me. . . . Ye are of your father the devil, and the lusts of your father ye will do. He was a murderer from the beginning, and abode not in the truth, because there is no truth in him." (John 8: 42-44.)

CURSE UPON THE JEWS

Can anyone say that in the subsequent history of the Jews, following their rejection and crucifixion of Jesus Christ, the curse pronounced upon the basket of bad figs has not been fulfilled to the letter upon this people? They have become a byword, a taunt and a proverb in all countries, "tossed to and fro" among the nations, and have been cursed and harassed as predicted. They continue even now under this condemnation in their continued rejection of Jesus Christ. Following the teachings of the Talmud, which Jesus described as the traditions of men, and which He condemned (Mark 7: 7-9), this people have been a seed of evil in all nations because they have refused to accept Jesus Christ as the Messiah and keep His commandments. Never has the history of any people shown a more noticeably accurate and literal fulfillment of published curses upon them than the history of the Jewish race, exemplified in the centuries of suffering and persecutions which they have had to endure. Nor are these days ended, for in their continued refusal to acknowledge the Messiahship of Jesus Christ they plan to take the Kingdom by force and occupy the land of Israel by violence. Their present attitude and acts will only increase and intensify their afflictions. The suffering of the Jew is in itself irrefutable evidence of the truth of prophecy, for the curse uttered by Jeremiah upon them and their children, and confirmed by the generation of our Lord's day who said, "His blood be on us, and on our children" (Matt. 27:25), is being intensified a thousand-fold in these latter days.

Jeremiah said to his generation:

"The Lord hath sent unto you all his servants the prophets, rising early and sending them; but ye have not harkened, nor inclined your ear to hear." (Jer. 25:4.)

Jesus declared that His generation were the children of them that killed the prophets and He said:

"Fill ye up then the measure of your fathers. Ye serpents, ye generation of vipers, how can ye escape the damnation of hell? Wherefore, behold, I send unto you prophets, and wise men, and scribes: and some of them ye shall kill and crucify; and some of them shall ye scourge in your synagogues, and persecute them from city to city: That upon you may come all the righteous blood shed upon the earth." (Matt. 23:32-35.)

In both generations, Jeremiah's and our Lord's, the people refused to hear or turn from their evil ways. Upon his generation Jeremiah declared God would send His servant Nebuchadnezzar, King of Babylon, that he would also destroy the nations around them, but they would serve the King of Babylon 70 years. At the end of the 70 years Babylon would be punished for her iniquity. Jesus pronounced the destruction of the Temple and city for His generation's rejection of Him and the prophecy was literally fulfilled in 70 A.D., when the armies of Rome devastated the land and burned the city and Temple.

WINE CUP OF FURY

God commissioned Jeremiah to give to all nations the wine cup of fury that they might be moved (shakened) and become mad because of the sword God sent among them. The prophet declares:

"Then took I the cup at the Lord's hand, and made all nations to drink, unto whom the Lord had sent me." (Jer. 25: 17.)

The nations have been mad ever since as they have warred one upon the other and the sword has slaughtered millions from the time Jeremiah was commanded to give this cup of fury to the nations to the present day. Beginning with Babylon, whose empire was succeeded by Medo-Persia, then Greece and Rome, and finally the continental powers, all have taken of the cup of wrath and have been "reeling to and fro," drunk with the wine of madness.

Jerusalem and the cities of Judah headed the list
of those to whom the cup was given, after which Jeremiah records the names of the nations and kingdoms
to partake of this wine of fury. Thus madness and violence are prophesied as beginning with Jerusalem and
spreading to the ends of the earth as God calls for a
sword upon all the inhabitants of the world. The scope
of this judgment covers the entire period of the Times
of the Gentiles, ending with the final overthrow of the
Kingdoms of this world. Jeremiah is told:

"Therefore prophesy thou against them all these
words, and say unto them, The Lord shall roar from
on high, and utter his voice from his holy habitation;
he shall mightily roar upon his habitation; he shall give
a shout, as they that tread the grapes, against all the
inhabitants of the earth." (Jer. 25: 30.)

Here, depicted in terms of the harvest, is shown the
execution of judgment upon the nations. It is couched
in language similar to that used by Joel when he speaks
of the events which would bring the age to an end. Joel
declared judgment has come and the wine press is full,
at which time the Lord will roar out of Zion, and utter
his voice from Jerusalem (Joel 3: 13-16).

Jeremiah is given a vision of war and turmoil during
the entire period of the Times of the Gentiles and beyond to the close of the age as God moves to finally put
the enemies of His Kingdom to rout:

"A noise shall come even to the ends of the earth:
for the Lord hath a controversy with the nations, he will
plead with all flesh; he will give them that are wicked

to the sword, saith the Lord. Thus saith the Lord of hosts, Behold, evil shall go forth from nation to nation, and a great whirlwind shall be raised up from the coasts of the earth. And the slain of the Lord shall be at that day from one end of the earth even unto the other end of the earth: they shall not be lamented, neither gathered, nor buried." (Jer. 25: 31-33.)

Here is succinctly revealed the disaster and destruction at the end of the age resulting from world-wide conflict. Already this prophecy is partially fulfilled in the events of World Wars I and II and complete fulfillment will come when Gog moves against His people Israel.

TROUBLED NATIONAL LEADERS

A message is next addressed to the heads of government, the rulers and leaders of the people, calling upon them to howl and the principal men to roll in ashes because the time for them to be slain has come. There was no escape for these rulers and no way for the principal men to flee. The prophet pointed out that their kingdoms and states would be wasted and the peaceful places destroyed. The fierce anger of the Lord was likened to a lion which has left his lair to make the country desolate. The series of judgments upon all nations was to continue without abatement because of evil oppression and the tyranny of the oppressor.

Jeremiah had been commissioned to stand in the court of the Lord's house, and to address those of the cities of Judah who came there to worship. He was to speak all the words he had been commanded to say and not omit a single word. If the people would repent of their evil ways, God would do good to them, but if they would not listen and turn from their evil ways then the Temple would be destroyed and Jerusalem become a city cursed in the sight of all nations.

Jeremiah ended his address, having spoken all which the Lord had commanded. Then the priests and preachers and all the people seized him, exclaiming, "You shall die!" They were highly incensed over his words that the House of the Lord would become as Shiloh and that Jerusalem would be burned and without inhabitants.

When the officials of Judah heard of it they went from the Palace to the House of the Lord and when court convened they sat down to judge Jeremiah at the new gate of the Lord's House. The Judges listened to the accusations brought by the priests and preachers against the prophet, who were claiming Jeremiah to be worthy of death because he had prophesied against the city. In his own defense Jeremiah declared:

"The Lord sent me to prophesy against this house and against this city all the words that ye have heard. Therefore now amend your ways and your doings, and obey the voice of the Lord your God; and the Lord will repent him of the evil that he hath pronounced against you. As for me, behold, I am in your hand: do with me as seemeth good and meet unto you. But know ye of a certain, that if ye put me to death, ye shall surely bring innocent blood upon yourself, and upon this city, and upon the inhabitants thereof: for of a truth the Lord hath sent me unto you to speak all these words in your ears." (Jer. 26: 12-15.)

The priests and preachers had preferred charges and the officials and judges in Judah were hearing the case. In his own cause Jeremiah made a masterly defense. He asserted he had prophesied by Divine command and appealed to the conscience of his judges, as well as to those who falsely accused him. Though he asserted he was ready to die, yet he warned the judges that if he was condemned to death they would be guilty of murdering an innocent man.

Consequently, the officials and the people told the priests and the preachers that there was no evidence which would warrant Jeremiah being condemned to death as he had spoken in the name of the Lord. A debate ensued and in defense of the prophet certain ones among the judges presented the following statement by the prophet Micah who had prophesied in the days of Hezekiah, King of Judah:

"Thus saith the Lord of hosts; Zion shall be plowed like a field, and Jerusalem shall become heaps, and the mountain of the house as the high places of a forest." (Jer. 26: 18; see also Micah 3: 12.)

The question was then asked and answered:

"Did Hezekiah king of Judah and all Judah put him at all to death? Did he not fear the Lord, and besought the Lord, and the Lord repented him of the evil which he had pronounced against them?" (Jer. 26: 19.)

Following this plea in behalf of Jeremiah, this defender of the prophet asked if the court should do this great wrong and slay an innocent man? The argument was closed in favor of sparing the prophet's life.

We are not told who set forth the case against Jeremiah and gave the argument in favor of putting him to death but we do know that the animosity of both the priests and preachers because of Jeremiah's prophecies could very readily stir one of their number to declare:

"And there was also a man that prophesied in the name of the Lord, Urijah the son of Shemaiah of Kirjath-jearim, who prophesied against this city and against this land according to all the words of Jeremiah: And when Jehoiakim the king, with all his mighty men, and all the princes, heard his words, the king sought to put him to death; but when Urijah heard it he was afraid, and fled, and went into Egypt; And Jehoiakim the king sent men into Egypt . . . And they fetched forth Urijah out of Egypt, and brought him unto Jehoiakim the king, who slew him with the sword, and cast his dead body into the graves of the common people." (Jer. 26: 20-23.)

This judgment of Jehoiakim, instead of that of Hezekiah, was urged by those accusing Jeremiah as the one which should be taken as a precedent by the court. Doing so, Jeremiah would be condemned to death.

But God had commissioned Jeremiah, not only to "root out, and to pull down, and to destroy, and to throw down," but he was also "to build, and to plant" (Jer. 1: 10). So his life must be spared and God raised up powerful friends for him, such as Ahikam, who favored the prophet and evidently pleaded his cause so successfully that he was not delivered up to be put to death but acquitted of the charges.

CHAPTER X

JEREMIAH'S CONTROVERSY WITH THE PREACHERS

The priests and prophets had failed in their attempt to have Jeremiah executed for prophesying against Jerusalem and the Temple. However, instead of letting the issue end (Jeremiah 26), the failure to convict Jeremiah increased the antagonism of the opposition as the false preachers began a campaign of falsification against him. It was their hope to so completely discredit Jeremiah and his prophecies that no one would listen to him or believe him.

An international conference of major importance was being held in Jerusalem at the beginning of Zedekiah's reign. During this conference the word of the Lord came to Jeremiah commanding him to deliver an important message to the ambassadors who had gathered for the meetings.

The authorized version of the Bible states this was in the beginning of the reign of Jehoiakim. In several of the older Mss., and in the Syriac version, it is stated to be Zedekiah and the contents of the chapter clearly indicates it was during the latter king's reign. Ferrar Fenton in a footnote says:

"In the ordinary text it is Jehoiakim, by a scribe's error—but Zedekiah in the original reading."

JEREMIAH MAKES YOKES

In the beginning of Zedekiah's reign, then, the word of the Lord came to Jeremiah instructing him to make yokes of thongs and bars. Leaving one upon his own neck, he sent the others with a message to the kings of Edom, Moab, Ammon, Tyre and Zidon by the hand of the ambassadors from those kingdoms who had come to Jerusalem to confer with Zedekiah.

FOREIGN AMBASSADORS

Evidently this foreign ministers' conference, being held at Jerusalem with ambassadors present from the nations mentioned above, was for the purpose of forming a league in order to resist the military advances of Nebuchadnezzar, King of Babylon. God instructed Jeremiah to take the yoke and place it upon his own neck in the sight of this delegation and command each to say to his master:

"Thus saith the Lord of hosts, the God of Israel; Thus shall ye say unto your masters; I have made the earth, the man and the beast that are upon the ground, by my great power and by my outstretched arm, and have given it unto whom it seemed meet unto me [or "I give it to whoever is upright in My sight" F. F. Trans.]." (Jer. 27: 4-5.)

These ambassadors of heathen nations were gathered at Jerusalem, no doubt with their best military advisors, to devise ways and means to combat Babylon. They were informed by Jeremiah that the God of Israel, the Creator of all things, was the One who would say who shall possess the earth. All their planning and schemes would come to naught unless approved of God. It would be well if this advice given by Jeremiah then would be heeded by the leaders of the nations today, for it is a fundamental fact that the God of Israel still rules in heaven and His desires will be carried out upon earth and evil aggressors brought to judgment. The earth is the Lord's and the fullness thereof and God has promised that Israel shall have the dominion. The way is even now being opened for Israel, chastised and cleansed of evil, to be restored to favor with God and through Him be used to bring about peace that righteousness may be established upon earth.

SUPREMACY OF BABYLON PREDICTED

In the name of Jehovah, the God of Israel, Jeremiah warned the ambassadors in attendance at Jerusalem to report to their respective masters:

"And now have I given all these lands into the hand of Nebuchadnezzar the king of Babylon, my servant; and the beasts of the field have I given him also to serve him. And all nations shall serve him, and his son, and his son's son, until the very time of his land come [i.e., until the time comes for his own land to be subjugated]; and then many nations and great kings shall serve themselves of him [or make him serve]." (Jer. 27: 6-7.)

WARNING AGAINST FALSE PROPHETS

Because the kings of the countries to which Jeremiah

was addressing this message had consulted with their mediums, necromancers and astrologers, the prophet warned them:

"Harken not ye to your prophets, nor to your diviners, nor to your dreamers, nor to your enchanters, nor to your sorcerers, which speak unto you, saying, Ye shall not serve the king of Babylon: For they prophesy a lie unto you, to remove you far from your land; and that I shall drive you out, and ye shall perish." (Jer. 27: 9-10.)

FUTILITY OF OPPOSITION

Jeremiah advised them how to avoid all this disaster—advice that was very likely far from acceptable:

"But the nations that bring their neck under the yoke of the king of Babylon, and serve him, those will I let remain still in their own land, saith the Lord; and they shall till it, and dwell therein." (Jer. 27: 11.)

Here we have a prophet of the Lord appearing before the ambassadors of many nations gathered in conference with a vital message from Jehovah, the God of Israel. They were warned of the futility of their plans to oppose the military advances of the King of Babylon and advised to submit to him. After addressing the foreign ambassadors Jeremiah turned to Zedekiah, King of Judah, and advised him to submit to Nebuchadnezzar and serve him. Evidently the attitude of the King indicated refusal to follow such counsel for Jeremiah asked the question:

"Why will ye die, thou and thy people, by the sword,

by the famine, and by the pestilence, as the Lord hath spoken against the nation that will not serve the king of Babylon?" (Jer. 27: 13.)

Just as the prophet had informed the ambassadors that their religious leaders were lying to them, so he tells Zedekiah:

"Hearken not unto the words of the prophets that speak unto you, saying, Ye shall not serve the king of Babylon: for they prophesy a lie unto you. For I have not sent them, saith the Lord, yet they prophesy a lie in my name." (Jer. 27: 14-15.)

LYING PROPHETS

Jeremiah knew that the false preachers were doing everything to flatter the king, telling him what he wanted to believe so Zedekiah would consider those his enemies who fearlessly told the truth. If, however, the King followed the advice of his lying preachers Jeremiah declared it would all end by his being driven out to perish, and the prophets as well would be destroyed who were using the name of the Lord falsely. The people and priests were told to refuse to listen to the false prophets who were saying the vessels of the Lord's house would be returned to Jerusalem. Jeremiah insisted:

"They prophesy a lie unto you. Hearken not unto them; serve the king of Babylon, and live: wherefore should this city be laid waste?" (Jer. 27: 16-17.)

TEST DEMANDED

This appeal was evidently falling upon deaf ears and

Jeremiah challenged the false prophets to make a test:

"If they be prophets, and if the word of the Lord be with them, let them now make intercession to the Lord of Hosts, that the vessels which are left in the house of the Lord, and in the house of the king of Judah, and at Jerusalem, go not to Babylon." (Jer. 27: 18.)

The vessels in the Temple were the constant object of care by the priests and Jeremiah, who had previously been brought before a tribunal for prophesying against Jerusalem and the Temple, declared that the sacred vessels would be carried away to Babylon:

"For thus saith the Lord of hosts concerning the pillars, and concerning the sea, and concerning the bases, and concerning the residue of the vessels that remain in this city, Which Nebuchadnezzar king of Babylon took not, when he carried away captive Jeconiah the son of Jehoiakim king of Judah from Jerusalem to Babylon, and all the nobles of Judah and Jerusalem; Yea, thus saith the Lord of hosts, the God of Israel, concerning the vessels that remain in the house of the Lord, and in the house of the king of Judah and of Jerusalem; They shall be carried away to Babylon, and there shall they be until the day that I visit them, saith the Lord: then will I bring them up, and restore them to this place." (Jer. 27: 19-22.)

Here we have a most interesting prophecy given as a result of the controversy Jeremiah was having with the priests and false prophets of his day. These spiritual leaders were challenged to intercede with God through prayer, if they were truly prophets of the Lord, and thus prevent the temple vessels from being carried away to Babylon. History has proved that they had no power with God for Jeremiah's prediction came to pass and all the vessels of the House of the Lord were carried away to Babylon.

AN INTERESTING UNFULFILLED PROPHECY

Jeremiah used this occasion not only to prophesy that the vessels would be taken away but to also prophesy of a day to come when they would be restored once more to Jerusalem. Somewhere, perhaps buried in the ruins of Ancient Babylon awaiting the day of discovery, are these furnishings of the Temple. Just as surely as the prophecy of their being carried away came to pass, so will the prophecy of their return be fulfilled.

There was a partial fulfillment of this prophecy when, following the seventy years of Babylonian Captivity, Ezra states:

"Also Cyrus the king brought forth the vessels of the house of the Lord, which Nebuchadnezzar had brought forth out of Jerusalem, and had put them in the house of his gods; Even those did Cyrus king of Persia bring forth by the hand of Mithredath the treasurer, and numbered them unto Sheshbazzar, the prince of Judah. And this is the number of them: thirty chargers of gold, a thousand chargers of silver, nine and twenty knives, thirty basons of gold, silver basons of a second sort four hundred and ten, and other vessels a thousand. All the vessels of gold and of silver were five thousand and four hundred. All these did Sheshbazzar bring up with them of the captivity that were brought up from Babylon unto Jerusalem." (Ezra 1: 7-11.)

Further reference is made to these temple furnishings in Ezra 5: 14 and I Esdras 2: 10-15. But this return of these vessels to the temple after the Babylonian Captivity did not include the restoration of the pillars of brass, the brazen sea and perhaps other temple furnishings which are yet to be returned in the coming day of complete restoration. From the ruins of Babylon, and from those places where they have disappeared from view, the brass, the gold and the silver will be brought forth once more and restored to Jerusalem.

HANANIAH'S PROPHECY

The boldness of Jeremiah in appearing before the ambassadors of the nations, who with Zedekiah were undertaking to form an alliance against Nebuchadnezzar, would necessarily be challenged by the false preachers of his day. The prophet had denounced the religious leaders, not only of the heathen nations whose representatives were present in Jerusalem, but also those in his own nation. The challenge was met by Hananiah, a prophet of Gibeon, who in the presence of the priests and people declared that the Lord of Hosts had broken the yoke of the King of Babylon and who predicted that the vessels of the Lord's house which Nebuchadnezzar had taken to Babylon would be brought back again. Also, he said that Jeconiah (*i.e.*, Jehoiachin or Coniah) the son of Jehoiakim, with all the rest of the captives in Babylon, would be brought back to Jerusalem again.

JEREMIAH'S REPLY

Jeremiah replied in the presence of the priests and all the people saying, "Amen," for he hoped that the Lord would do all Hananiah declared. There was no desire on Jeremiah's part that his people suffer, but in considering Hananiah's prophecy he asked the priests and people to reconcile his message of peace with the following facts. He addressed Hananiah:

"The prophets that have been before me and before thee or old [such as Isaiah, Micah, Amos, Joel, etc.], prophesied both against many countries and against great kingdoms, of war, and of evil, and of pestilence." (Jer. 28:8.)

Hananiah's statement was in complete contrast to the words of all these prophets for he declared peace would surely come, and soon. Jeremiah said to the priests and people:

"The prophet which prophesieth of peace [the blessings of restoration], when the word of the prophet shall come to pass, then shall the prophet be known, that the Lord hath truly sent him." (Jer. 28:9.)

HANANIAH BREAKS THE YOKE

Hananiah's reply to this statement was to take the yoke off Jeremiah's neck and break it, saying:

"Thus saith the Lord; Even so will I break the yoke

of Nebuchadnezzar king of Babylon from the neck of all nations within the space of two full years." (Jer. 28: 11.)

Jeremiah made no reply but went his way. He was dealing with one who had claimed to represent the Lord and in whose name he had spoken. Until God commissioned the prophet to make a reply he could do nothing but accept the words of Hananiah. He therefore remained silent. Jeremiah was not in a position to argue with the people against the prophecy because it had been spoken in the name of the Lord.

HANANIAH'S DEATH PREDICTED

But the word of the Lord came to Jeremiah saying:

"Go and tell Hananiah, saying, Thus saith the Lord; Thou hast broken the yokes of wood; but thou shalt make for them yokes of iron." (Jer. 28: 13-14.)

Hananiah's opposition to Jeremiah before the foreign ambassadors and in front of the priests and people made him responsible for their refusal to listen to the truth. This also made him directly responsible for the yokes of iron which their refusal to listen to Jeremiah would bring upon their necks. God declared that yokes of iron would be placed upon the necks of all nations for they would indeed serve the King of Babylon. Jeremiah then addressed a personal message to Hananiah:

"Here now, Hananiah, the Lord hath not sent thee; but thou makest this people to trust in a lie. Therefore thus saith the Lord, Behold, I will cast thee from off the face of the earth: this year thou shalt die, because thou hast taught rebellion against God." (Jer. 28: 15-16.)

This judgment may seem severe but Hananiah, by pretending to speak in the name of the Lord, had turned the people away from the truth. He had taught opposition to the Lord by his lies and encouraged the people to disbelieve the word of the Lord, causing them to revolt against God. Hananiah, the prophet, died in the same year in accordance with the prediction of Jeremiah.

LETTER TO CAPTIVES IN BABYLON

A letter was addressed by Jeremiah to the captives who were carried away to Babylon after Jeconiah (Jehoiakin or Coniah) and the people who were with him had been carried away from Jerusalem. This letter was entrusted to the messenger who was sent by Zedekiah, King of Judah, to Nebuchadnezzar to renew his promises of fidelity. In his letter to the captives Jeremiah instructed them:

"Build ye houses, and dwell in them; and plant gardens, and eat the fruit of them; Take ye wives, and beget sons and daughters; and take wives for your sons, and give your daughters to husbands, that they may bear sons and daughters; that ye may be increased there, and not diminished. And seek [plead for] the peace of the city whither I have caused you to be carried away captives, and pray unto the Lord for it: for in the peace thereof shall ye have peace." (Jer. 29: 5-7.)

The captives in Babylon were to prepare for a long stay in the land of their captors. Evidently there were those among them in Babylon who were stirring up the people into a state of constant mental agitation by promises of an early return to their native land. In order to offset these foolish prophecies and prevent the raising of false hopes, Jeremiah wrote to warn the people against listening to the would-be prophets in their midst:

"Let not your prophets and your diviners, that be in the midst of you, deceive you, neither hearken to your dreams which ye cause to be dreamed. For they prophesy falsely unto you in my name; I have not sent them, saith the Lord." (Jer. 29: 8-9.)

The duration of their captivity was then given:

"For thus saith the Lord, That after seventy years be accomplished at Babylon I will visit you, and perform my good will toward you, in causing you to return to this place." (Jer. 29: 10.)

A MESSAGE OF COMFORT

This message of the prophet doomed many who had been carried away to Babylon to death in the land of their captors, without hope or ever again seeing their native land. But the message also provided an incentive to build and work that they might make the most of the opportunities which would come to them in the land of their captors. If they would obey the prophet's injunction and settle down in the land, build, plant and reap, as well as carry on the normal family life, there would be hope of their children's return to the land of

their fathers. A message of comfort was also addressed
to them:

"For I know the thoughts that I think toward you,
saith the Lord, thoughts of peace, and not of evil, to
give you an expected end. Then shall ye call upon me,
and ye shall go and pray unto me, and I will hearken
unto you. And ye shall seek me, and find me, when ye
shall search for me with all your heart." (Jer. 29:
11-13.)

THE VILE FIGS

Following this, the promise of restoration was given.
Of Zedekiah, however, who was sitting upon the
Throne of David, and of their brethren who were
dwelling in Jerusalem and as yet had not gone into
captivity, Jeremiah declared:

"Thus saith the Lord of hosts; Behold, I will send
upon them the sword, the famine, and the pestilence,
and will make them like vile figs, that cannot be eaten,
they are so evil." (Jer. 29: 17.)

This is followed by the repetition of the curse upon
the basket of bad figs—those of Judah who were to be
persecuted with sword, famine and pestilence. They
were to be removed to all the kingdoms of the earth to
be a curse, an astonishment, a hissing and a reproach
among all nations where they would be driven. The
reason given by the prophet is:

"Because they have not hearkened to my words, saith
the Lord, which I sent unto them by my servants the

prophets, rising up early and sending them." (Jer. 29: 19.)

JUDGMENT UPON FALSE PROPHETS

Jeremiah counseled the exiles in Babylon not to do as the people at Jerusalem were doing; that is, refuse to listen to and heed the words of the Lord. Though they had self-styled prophets at Babylon, such as Ahab and Zedekiah, Jeremiah declared:

"Thus saith the Lord of hosts, the God of Israel, of Ahab the son of Kolaiah, and of Zedekiah the son of Maaseiah, which prophesy a lie unto you in my name; Behold, I will deliver them into the hand of Nebuchadnezzar king of Babylon; and he will slay them before your eyes." (Jer. 29: 21.)

It should be remembered that Daniel held an important position in the court of Babylon at that time and was close to Nebuchadnezzar, the King. Jeremiah's letters would be of great interest to Daniel and the prophet's mention of the seditious acts of Ahab and Zedekiah would very likely be called to Nebuchadnezzar's attention. Thus Jeremiah, by mentioning the judgment to come upon the two false prophets, actually signed their death warrants, for Nebuchadnezzar was very kindly disposed toward him and would act upon his advice.

JEREMIAH CALLED A MADMAN

Shemaiah, a dreamer who was with the captives at Babylon, wrote a letter on his own account to Zephaniah, who was next to the High Priest at Jerusalem, and to all the priests, demanding that as a priest he ought to put every madman who posed as a prophet into prison and in the stocks. He wanted to know why he had not reprimanded Jeremiah of Anathoth? He had been posing as a prophet and had sent word to Babylon that the exile would be long and that they were to build houses and live in them and plant gardens and eat the produce of them.

Zephaniah, the priest, read the letter to Jeremiah and the word of the Lord came to Jeremiah saying:

"Send to all them of the captivity, saying, Thus saith the Lord concerning Shemaiah the Nehelamite [dreamer]; Because that Shemaiah hath prophesied unto you, and I sent him not, and he caused you to trust in a lie: Therefore thus saith the Lord; Behold, I will punish Shemaiah the Nehelamite, and his seed: he shall not have a man to dwell among this people; neither shall he behold the good that I will do for my people, saith the Lord; because he hath taught rebellion against the Lord." (Jer. 29: 31-32.)

GOD'S ENEMIES

One of the outstanding results in this controversy between Jeremiah and those who tried to destroy him and his work was that the vengeance they planned against Jeremiah boomeranged upon their own heads. God was with the prophet and his enemies became God's enemies. Thus those who elected to fight him found they were fighting against God. Judgment was passed upon them and God commissioned Jeremiah to render that judgment. The prophet's enemies had failed utterly in securing the conviction they hoped for when they forced Jeremiah to be tried in court and, following that, their vindictiveness against his person was rewarded by God Himself who moved swiftly to avenge the wrongs they committed against His servant, Jeremiah the prophet.

CHAPTER XI

THE NEW COVENANT

Evidence of the certainty of inspiration of the Scriptures is furnished in the instruction given by God to Jeremiah: "Write thee all the words that I have spoken unto thee in a book." (Jer. 30: 2). They were not to be left to the uncertainty of human memory and the reason for that was that the message of the Lord was not only addressed to the men and women of Jeremiah's time but it had a profound prophetic significance for coming generations. The particular message the prophet was told to write in a book had to do with events in the latter days. Hence the message itself would become more understandable to future generations than to the generation of Jeremiah's time. The importance of the message required that it be preserved throughout the centuries so that those who would be living in the latter days might read and understand. Emphasis, therefore, is placed upon the importance of the message Jeremiah is told to preserve by the declaration that it is to be written down in a book, followed by the statement of fact by the Lord:

"For lo, the days come, saith the Lord, that I will bring again the captivity of my people Israel and Judah, saith the Lord; and I will cause them to return to the land that I gave to their fathers, and they shall possess it." (Jer. 30: 3.)

THE GREAT DAY OF THE LORD

Looking forward to the day when both Israel and Judah shall be restored, not only to their own land, but when they will live again in God's sight, a people cleansed of evil, Jeremiah sets forth the order of events leading to that restoration:

"For thus saith the Lord; We have heard a voice of trembling, of fear, and not of peace." (Jer. 30: 5.)

This description of a time when men would be in fear and not peace is prophetic of the conditions to prevail in the earth and among His people just prior to the great and terrible day of the Lord. The message continues as the evil and troubles of that time are described:

"Ask ye now, and see whether a man doth travail with child? wherefore do I see every man with his hands on his loins, as a woman in travail, and all faces are turned into paleness?" (Jer. 30: 6.)

TIME OF JACOB'S TROUBLE

The conditions of the times were to be so severe with increased suffering, misery and anguish that men would appear in great pain, like a woman about to give birth to a child. The cause of all this sorrow will be the events of the great and terrible day of the Lord designated by the prophet as the time of Jacob's trouble:

"Alas! for that day is great, so that none is like it: it is even the time of Jacob's trouble, but he shall be saved out of it." (Jer. 30: 7.)

The time of all this is when the power of Great Babylon will be broken as clearly indicated in the context. Ferrar Fenton translates the last clause of the above verse as a question: "Can he be saved from it?" The answer is:

"Yes! in that day, says the Ever-living, 'I will break the yoke from off your neck, and snap the shackles, and they shall no longer serve the foreigners, but serve their Ever-living God, and David their king whom I will appoint for them.'" (Jer. 30: 8-9, *F. F. Trans.*)

Two major facts here set forth are descriptive of the events of the great day of the Lord. The first deals with Jacob in distress and this period of difficulty is called "Jacob's trouble" from which Israel is to be finally saved. The second has to do with judgment upon all of Israel's enemies with the result that the foreigner will rule no more over God's people.

A PERIOD OF DISTRESS

The reference to Jacob's trouble immediately reminds one of the troubles Jacob himself experienced in serving for his wives, his meeting with his brother Esau when he returned from his sojourn with Laban, and the later mourning for Joseph whom he thought was dead.

One of the interesting factors in a study of the Scriptures is the events in the lives of Bible personalities, for they are often a type and their lives symbolic of events to take place in the future. The difficulties Jacob faced in his lifetime have a definite application to the difficulties and troubles his descendants would experience in the latter days. Jeremiah designates the troubles to come upon the descendants of Jacob as the age comes to a close as "even the time of Jacob's trouble."

What was his trouble? His first period of trouble was physical suffering which began with his flight from his father's home, his experience at the brook Jabbok when Esau was coming to meet him with four hundred men, ending at Bethel where he cleansed his household of all idolatry. The duration of this first period of trouble was 22 years. A second period of difficulty and trouble—one of mental anguish rather than physical suffering—is recorded as beginning when his son Joseph was sold by his brethren into slavery and Jacob mourned for him, believing him to be dead until 22 years later he met him in Egypt. Together, these two periods total 44 years, the exact number of years the Great Pyramid assigns for the consummation of the age, the chronology of which indicates its beginning in 1909 A.D. and ending in 1953 A.D. There are striking parallels between the 44 years of Jacob's distress and the events which have already become history since the beginning of the consummation of the age in 1909 A.D. We have witnessed the physical and mental suffering of the Israel people and at this writing seven years remain before the consummation is completed. Regardless of the stress and trouble yet to come, God has promised that Jacob shall be saved out of it—not from it—as final judgment is meted out to all the enemies of Israel.

ISRAEL'S REPENTANCE

Will there yet be repeated in the lifetime of the

present generation, in the coming move of Gog described in the 38th and 39th chapters of Ezekiel, the fulfillment upon the present-day descendants of Jacob of the mental and spiritual anguish he experienced at the brook Jabbok which led to his complete surrender to God? If this is so, then as a result of the helpless situation in which modern Israel will find herself when Russia moves, there will come a wide-spread spiritual awakening and whole-hearted turning to God for deliverance as Jacob had to turn to God before he was delivered from the fury of his brother Esau.

END OF BABYLONIAN RULE

Now the Babylonian yoke, which Jeremiah declared would be placed upon the neck of all nations, was to be broken off the neck of Israel at the time when His people would be delivered from their trouble. We have already witnessed judgment upon the Babylonian Succession of Empires with the end of Gentile rule brought about in the defeat of Germany and the unconditional surrender of the Nazis. Thus the political and military power of Babylon has fallen.* There remains only the completion of that judgment upon the economic and religious activities of Babylon to complete the removal of the yoke of bondage under which Israel has labored for many centuries. Along with this judgment upon Babylon, God promises to destroy the rule of the foreigners within Israel. We can thus look to the soon removal of alien rule in our midst through tribulation

* See "End of Gentile Rule," DESTINY for July, 1945.

and the destruction of those forces which would foist upon us forms of administration and government contrary to our Israel institutions.

DAVID, THEIR KING

According to Jeremiah we are to be brought back to God and serve the Lord. Then "David their king," whom Jeremiah declares God will raise up for us to serve, is none other than Jesus, the Christ. *David* signifies *beloved* which is the name God gave to His Son:

"And Jesus, when he was baptized, went up straightway out of the water; and, lo, the heavens were opened unto him, and he [John] saw the Spirit of God descending like a dove, and lighting upon him: And lo a voice from heaven, saying, This is my beloved [David] Son, in whom I am well pleased." (Matt. 3: 16-17.)

It is He and He only who will be able to bring salvation to the House of Israel and deliver them from the power of their enemies. As our father Jacob finally turned to God at the brook Jabbok and was delivered from destruction, so will modern Jacob turn to God as they face the attack from Gog of the land of Magog whose purpose is the destruction of God's people. But that deliverance will only come when Israel awakens spiritually as Jacob awakened after wrestling all night with the Angel and became willing to make restoration. Thus, modern Israel must become ready and willing to restore the administration of the Divine law. Then, and then only, will His people become rulers with Him and no more will they be called Jacob, the supplanter, but Israel, which means ruling with God!

A MESSAGE OF COMFORT

Because of the severity of the times as the enemies of Israel gather for the conflict which they expect will bring the annihilation of modern Israel as a nation in the world today, God admonishes His people:

"Therefore fear thou not, O my servant Jacob, saith the Lord; neither be dismayed, O Israel: for, lo, I will save thee from afar, and thy seed from the land of their captivity; and Jacob shall return and shall be in rest, and be quiet, and none shall make him afraid." (Jer. 30: 10.)

This is a message directed to Israel of the latter days as she faces an unscrupulous enemy preparing to destroy her. The prophet promises deliverance and, though Israel must suffer in measure for her sins, the Lord declares:

"I am with thee, saith the Lord, to save thee: though I make a full end of all nations whither I have scattered thee, yet I will not make a full end of thee: but I will correct thee in measure, and will not leave thee altogether unpunished." (Jer. 30: 11.)

PUNISHED IN MEASURE

The reason why Israel is punished in a measure is set forth by Jeremiah who chided Israel for lamenting over their afflictions and pointed out that all they had suffered had come upon them for the multitude of their iniquities and because their sins were increased. God allowed punishment to come upon Israel but he also declares:

"All they that devour thee shall be devoured; and all thine adversaries, every one of them, shall go into captivity; and they that spoil thee shall be a spoil, and all that prey upon thee will I give to the prey. For I will restore health unto thee, and I will heal thee of thy wounds." (Jer. 30: 16-17.)

UNDERSTANDING IN THE LATTER DAYS

God promises that Zion (Israel's government), despised by everyone, will be restored in the sight of all peoples and that the House of Jacob will return and strangers or aliens will rule over them no more. Then His people will approach Him with all their hearts and they will be, in fact as well as in name, His people and He will be their God. The prophet exclaims:

"Look! the furious tempest of the anger of the Lord has gone out! A sweeping tempest, it whirls over the head of the wicked. The flaming wrath of the Everliving will not return until it has accomplished the purpose of His heart." (Jer. 30: 23-24, *F. F. Trans.*)

Then comes the promise, "You will understand it in the future times, at the period." That will be the day when Gog of the land of Magog moves to destroy Israel for at that time God's fury will come up in His face:

"And it shall come to pass at the same time when Gog shall come against the land of Israel, saith the Lord God, that my fury shall come up in my face. For in my

jealousy and in the fire of my wrath have I spoken."
(Ez. 38: 18-19.)

This is followed by the description of a titanic earth-
quake and the complete destruction of the enemies of
our Lord and His Kingdom. All this is to be clearly
understood by Israel in the latter days or, as Ferrar
Fenton translates, "at the period." The Lord declares:

"At the same time [following the destruction of
Israel's enemies], saith the Lord, will I be the God of
all the families of Israel, and they shall be my people."
(Jer. 31: 1.)

This will result in:

"So the house of Israel shall know that I am the Lord
their God from that day and forward." (Ez. 39: 22.)

In order that the people of the covenant may know
their identity in the last days:

"Thus saith the Lord, The people which were left
of the sword found grace in the wilderness; even Israel,
when I went to cause him to rest." (Jer. 31: 2.)

Through Jeremiah God is here maintaining that
Israel was to find grace; that is, become a Christian people when far away from the land of Palestine and in
the wilderness of the people (Ez. 20: 35). Thus, one
of the major marks of identification by which Israel is
to be known in these latter days is that they are to be a
Christian people in accordance with Hosea's declaration
following the pronouncement that they would become
"not God's people":

"Yet the number of the children of Israel shall be
as the sand of the sea, which cannot be measured nor

numbered; and it shall come to pass, that in the place where it was said unto them, Ye are not my people, there it shall be said unto them, Ye are the sons of the living God [a Christian people]." (Hosea 1: 10.)

FATHER TO ISRAEL

God then declares His love for His people and that He will draw them to him with loving kindness. They are to be built again and become the head of nations. While they were carried away in tears, they are to return as a great multitude, walking in a path in which they will not stumble. For God affirms that He will be a Father to Israel, and Ephraim is His first-born. A proclamation is given:

"Nations! hear the message of the Lord, and report it to the distant isles, and proclaim it to the race of Israel, 'He who scattered us will guard you as a shepherd does his flock!' For the Ever-living will redeem Jacob and free him from the hand that is stronger than his." (Jer. 31: 10-11, *F. F. Trans.*)

PROSPERITY AND PEACE

Following this proclamation is the promise of the goodness of the Lord, for Israel is to be blessed with plenty of wheat, wine and oil and an increase in their flocks and herds. They will never again have to endure hardship and distress:

"Then the girls will rejoice in the dance, with the boys and old men with them. And I will change their sorrow to delight, and their sighing and anguish to gladness, and satiate their priests with fat, and fill my People with benefits, says the Ever-living." (Jer. 31:13-14. *F. F. Trans.*)

Prosperity, happiness and all the benefits of peace are to be the lot of Israel in the great restoration, which will follow the defeat of all their enemies and the destruction of alien rule over them.

CHILDREN SLAIN

Jeremiah refers prophetically to the slaughter of the children by Herod when he slew all children two years old and under in an endeavor to destroy Jesus Christ:

"Thus saith the Lord, A voice was heard in Ramah, lamentation, and bitter weeping; Rahel [Rachel] weeping for her children refused to be comforted for her children, because they were not." (Jer. 31:15.)

This prophecy was literally fulfilled and Matthew cites this passage (Matt. 2:17-18) as foretelling Herod's slaying of all the children in Bethlehem and in its vicinity. Rachel is mentioned for it was here that she died at the birth of her son Benjamin (Gen. 35:16-19).

PROMISE OF THE RESURRECTION

"Thus saith the Lord, Refrain thy voice from weeping, and thine eyes from tears: for thy work will be rewarded, saith the Lord; and they shall come again from the land of the enemy. And there is hope in thine end, saith the Lord, that thy children shall come again to their own border." (Jer. 31:16-17.)

God is here promising that through the resurrection, when the time of the restitution of all things has come, those who were thus slain will return to the land of the living. The injustice done will be rectified and those who have passed into the grave will live again. From the land of the enemy the children will return and this should be a comfort to all those who have lost members of their family through death.

GOD'S SON EPHRAIM

Ephraim is referred to as murmuring and complaining under chastisement like a bullock unaccustomed to the yoke. Though goaded and chastised, yet in exile Ephraim will have repented and desire to return to the Lord. In anticipation of the return to God, when Israel will repent, reference is made to Jacob's repentance at the brook Jabbok. Here Jacob, after the night of wrestling with the Angel, became lame (Gen. 32: 25). So Israel is prophetically made to say:

"I smote upon my thigh: I was ashamed, yea, even confounded, because I did bear the reproach of my youth." (Jer. 31: 19.)

MARKS OF IDENTIFICATION

God declares that Ephraim is His dear son, a pleasant child, and though it was necessary to speak sharply to him in the past, yet He loves him with the tenderest affection and admonishes him to:

"Set thee up way-marks, make thee high heaps: set thine heart toward the highway, even the way which thou wentest: turn again, O virgin of Israel, turn again to these thy cities." (Jer. 31: 21.)

Ferrar Fenton translates this:

"Set up your beacons—your Landmarks set up! Fix your heart on the mounds by the way that you marched, Return, Israel's daughter, return to your city."

Moffatt renders this passage:

"Put up waymarks, set up guideposts, bethink you of the high road, by which you travelled hence. Come back by it, O maiden Israel, come back to your home towns here."

After having declared Israel's coming wonderful blessings and God's protection over them, the call is for latter-day Israel to retrace the course over which they traveled westward. They were to leave beacons or waymarks along the way for latter-day guides that they might map the road over which they had trekked during the intervening centuries. Isaiah had the same thought in mind when he addressed the following message to a people who had lost the knowledge of their origin:

"Hearken to me, ye that follow after righteousness, ye that seek the Lord: look unto the rock whence ye are hewn, and to the hole of the pit whence ye are digged. Look unto Abraham your father, and unto Sarah that bare you: for I called him alone, and blessed him, and increased him." (Isa. 51: 1-2.)

SEARCHING THE RECORD

This message is addressed to a people who have forgotten that Abraham and Sarah were their ancestors. Having forgotten this fact they have also lost the knowledge of their origin. Isaiah is calling upon a people who follow righteousness, therefore a Christian nation, to recognize that they are Israel. Jeremiah declares that this same people, whom he states found grace in the wilderness, will study the many waymarks and evidences of identification as they trace their origin back over the highway to the cities of their forefathers and their origin as a kingdom at Mount Sinai. The call is for latter-day Israel to carefully and systematically search the records and this the Anglo-Saxon-Celtic peoples have been doing during the past century.

Never in the history of any people, other than the Anglo-Saxons, has there been such an interest taken in a knowledge of their origin. Present-day literature abounds with the results of such research, while the evidence furnished by the waymarks along the highway over which Israel marched in their westward trek through the centuries proves beyond question that the Anglo-Saxon-Celtic peoples are modern Israel. The very fact that they have carried out the instructions given to Israel to search the records of their origin is another mark to be added to the many which already prove them to be God's people. Abraham has taken his rightful place in his relation to this race, for millions have now come into a knowledge of the evidence supplied by painstaking research, revealing to them their father Abraham, and Sarah, their mother.

A HESITANT PEOPLE

Israel has now returned to the land of their forefathers, for Israel-Britain has come into the possession of Palestine and its cities. That branch of the House of Israel is in possession of their ancient homeland once more. The prophet prophetically asks how long Israel will hesitate for, though their identity has been proclaimed, millions among Israel refuse to accept the fact and believe they are God's people. Not only are the unchurched multitudes ignorant of the facts concerning this identification, but many of the leaders in the Church itself refuse to approach the subject in the spirit of an honest, unbiased, sincere investigator, checking the evidence against Scripture. If they would do so, it would prove beyond question the identity of the Anglo-Saxon-Celtic peoples with Israel of old. The origin, destiny and responsibility of the Anglo-Saxon-Celtic peoples, in the light of the marks designating them as Israel today, should awaken this people from their present state of spiritual lethargy. There should be no further hesitation on the part of modern Israel to awaken to the significance of the waymarks and guides revealing the road they have traveled since their ·organization into a Kingdom at Mount Sinai. The Lord makes a startling statement concerning the backsliding daughter of Israel:

ISRAEL, THE SUITOR

"For the Lord hath created a new thing in the earth, A woman shall compass a man." (Jer. 31: 22.)

Ferrar Fenton translates this:

"The Lord has prepared a new thing,
In that land, a woman embracing a man!"

Moffatt renders this:

"Why, the Eternal makes a new thing upon earth; frail woman becomes manly!"

There have been many conjectures about the meaning of this passage. It is to be noted, however, that the prophet is referring to the erring daughter of Israel and therefore it has to do with this same maiden, daughter, or virgin of Israel who is to compass (turn about so as to return to and seek the favor of) a man. Thus, the woman becomes the suitor; that is, becomes manly, as the virgin of Israel seeks the Lord, the Mighty One of Israel.

When the Lord restores the fortunes of His people who have returned to Him:

"They shall again say this thing in the land of Judah and in its cities when I restore you from captivity, 'The Ever-living bless you, Home of righteousness, Hill of Holiness!' For Judah shall reside in it, and all his cities,—together with farmers, and the shepherds of flocks, when I will refresh the weary life, and fill every exhausted soul." (Jer. 31: 23-26, *F. F. Trans.*)

TO BUILD AND TO PLANT

Jeremiah's mission had been one of destruction as he prophesied that calamity would come upon calamity for those who dwelt in the land of Palestine. But God had also commissioned him to "build and to plant." This latter part of his mission was to be accomplished elsewhere, not in Palestine. Looking forward to the process of building and planting, the Lord said:

"Behold, the days come, saith the Lord, that I will sow the house of Israel, and the house of Judah with the seed of man, and with the seed of beast. And it shall come to pass, that like as I have watched over them, to pluck up, and to break down, and to throw down, and to destroy, and to afflict [all of which had been taking place in Palestine, both upon Israel and Judah, as well as upon the city of Jerusalem]; so will I watch over them, to build, and to plant, saith the Lord." (Jer. 31: 27-28.)

Jeremiah was given the task to lay the foundation of the building and planting after he left Palestine. We will deal later with the history of this phase of his work which must have been to him the most important part of his mission.

As a result of the new covenant which God is to make with His people, He declares the children will not die any more for the sins of their fathers but every one will be judged according to his own acts.

THE NEW COVENANT

"Behold, the days come, saith the Lord, that I will make a new covenant with the house of Israel, and with the house of Judah." (Jer. 31: 31).

Let it be noted that this New Covenant is to be made with no people other than Israel and Judah. It is not to be according to the covenant made with them when God led them out of Egypt, which they had broken, although the Lord declared he had been a husband to them. However, it must not be overlooked that in the second clause the House of Israel alone is mentioned:

"This shall be the covenant that I will make with the house of Israel; After those days, saith the Lord, I will put my law in their inward parts, and write it in their hearts; and will be their God, and they shall be my people." (Jer. 31: 33.)

THE MESSENGER OF THE COVENANT

Later on, Jesus Christ, as the Messenger of the Covenant, came in fulfillment of Malachi's prophecy:

"And the Lord whom ye seek, shall suddenly come to his temple, even the messenger of the covenant, whom ye delight in: behold, he shall come, saith the Lord of hosts." (Malachi 3: 1.)

As the Messenger of the Covenant, Jesus Christ wrote the terms of the New Covenant as set forth in His instructions to His disciples. The law, which before had been kept under the terms of the Old Covenant as an outward demonstration, is now made a matter of keeping the law inwardly, in heart relationship. Jesus illustrated this when He said:

"Ye have heard that it was said by them of old time, Thou shalt not kill; and whosoever shall kill shall be in danger of the judgment: But I say unto you, That whosoever is angry with his brother without a cause shall be in danger of the judgment." (Matt. 5: 21-22.)

Again Jesus said:

"Ye have heard that it was said by them of old time, Thou shalt not commit adultery: But I say unto you,

That whosoever looketh on a woman to lust after her hath committed adultery with her already in his heart." (Matt. 5: 27-28.)

LAW UNCHANGED

Jesus in no way changed the law but He did show that the same law, under the New Covenant, must be kept by all those who followed Him, but in a heart relationship, and so He told His disciples:

"That except your righteousness [your keeping of the law] shall exceed the righteousness of the scribes and Pharisees, ye shall in no case enter into the kingdom of heaven." (Matt. 5: 20.)

Paul cites Jeremiah's statement regarding the New Covenant and declares it was fulfilled in the coming of Jesus Christ who set forth its terms. In the day that all Israel accepts the terms of the New Covenant, when every man will keep His laws, Israel will walk in accordance with all His statutes and judments, at which time God declares:

"And they shall teach no more every man his neighbour, and every man his brother, saying, Know the Lord: for they shall all know me, from the least of them unto the greatest of them saith the Lord: for I will forgive their iniquity, and I will remember their sin no more." (Jer. 31: 34.)

A NEW HEART

This is in conformity with the message of the Lord to the House of Israel as spoken by Ezekiel:

"For I will take you from among the heathen, and

gather you out of all countries, and will bring you into your own land. Then will I sprinkle clean water upon you, and ye shall be clean: from all your filthiness, and from all your idols, will I cleanse you. A new heart also will I give you, and a new spirit will I put within you: and I will take away the stony heart out of your flesh, and I will give you an heart of flesh. And I will put my spirit within you, and cause you to walk in my statutes, and ye shall keep my judgments, and do them. And ye shall dwell in the land that I gave to your fathers: and ye shall be my people, and I will be your God." (Ezekiel 36: 24-28.)

ONE NATION

Referring to the results to follow the cleansing of the House of Israel of all her sins, the Lord says:

"And I will make them one nation in the land upon the mountains of Israel; and one king shall be king to them all: and they shall be no more two nations, neither shall they be divided into two kingdoms any more at all; Neither shall they defile themselves any more with their idols, nor with their detestable things, nor with any of their transgressions: but I will save them out of all their dwellingplaces, wherein they have sinned, and will cleanse them: so shall they be my people, and I will be their God. And David my servant shall be king over them; and they shall have one shepherd: they shall also walk in my judgments and observe my statutes and do them . . . Moreover I will make a covenant of peace with them; it shall be an everlasting covenant with them: and I will place them, and multiply them, and will set my sanctuary in the midst of them for evermore. My tabernacle also shall be with them: yea, I will be their God, and they shall be my people. And the heathen shall know that I the Lord do sanctify Israel, when my sanctuary shall be in the midst of them for evermore." (Ezekiel 37: 22-28.)

A NATION CONTINUALLY

Following the prophecy of the giving of a New Covenant, God assures Jeremiah that Israel shall never cease to be a nation before Him:

"Thus saith the Lord, which giveth the sun for a light by day, and the ordinances of the moon and of the stars for a light by night, which divideth the sea when the waves thereof roar; The Lord of hosts is his name: If those ordinances depart from before me, saith the Lord, then the seed of Israel also shall cease from being a nation before me for ever. Thus saith the Lord; If heaven above can be measured, and the foundations of the earth searched out beneath, I will also cast off all the seed of Israel for all that they have done, saith the Lord." (Jer. 31: 35-37.)

The ordinances of heaven are still functioning; the sun shines by day and the moon by night, so Israel must be a nation in the world today. Because this people as yet have not awakened to the knowledge of their origin, they not only remain unrecognized as yet by the world at large but are unknown to themselves. In the great deliverance that will be wrought when the enemies of

His Kingdom attack under the leadership of Gog, Ezekiel declares:

"So the house of Israel shall know that I am the Lord their God from that day and forward." (Ezekiel 39: 22.)

CAPITAL OF THE KINGDOM

Following the declaration that the House of Israel shall be a nation forever before Him, God declares of the city of Jerusalem, which was about to be destroyed in Jeremiah's time:

"Behold, the days come, saith the Lord, that the city shall be built to the Lord from the tower of Hananeel unto the gate of the corner. And the measuring line shall yet go forth over against it upon the hill Gareb, and shall compass about to Goath. And the whole valley of the dead bodies, and of the ashes, and all the fields unto the brook of Kidron, unto the corner of the horse gate toward the east, shall be holy unto the Lord; it shall not be plucked up, nor thrown down any more for ever." (Jer. 31: 38-40.)

The broad lines thus laid out are part of the plan by which the city of Jerusalem, the capital of the spiritually rejuvenated Kingdom, is to be rebuilt in the latter days. Already Jerusalem is spreading out to include the territory defined by the prophet. The complete fulfillment will become an acknowledged fact when the restoration of Israel is achieved, following the great spiritual awakening which will bring God's people into full favor with Him again.

CHAPTER XII

THE DAVIDIC COVENANT CONFIRMED

Zedekiah, King of Judah, imprisoned Jeremiah because of the prophecies he had uttered against Judah, Jerusalem and the King. The armies of the King of Babylon had begun to lay siege to Jerusalem at the time Jeremiah was put in prison. This was the tenth year of Zedekiah's reign and the eighteenth year of the reign of Nebuchadnezzar. It was the year 3415 A.M., dating from Adam, or 581 B.C.

Zedekiah was very much disturbed by the utterances of Jeremiah who had prophesied:

"Thus saith the Lord, Behold, I will give this city into the hand of the king of Babylon, and he shall take it; And Zedekiah king of Judah shall not escape out of the hand of the Chaldeans, but shall surely be delivered into the hand of the king of Babylon, and shall speak with him mouth to mouth, and his eyes shall behold his eyes; And he shall lead Zedekiah to Babylon, and there shall he be until I visit him, saith the Lord: though ye fight with the Chaldeans, ye shall not prosper." (Jer. 32: 3-5.)

Ezekiel had also prophesied the course of Zedekiah's life, declaring he would not see Babylon (Ez. 12: 13). Both Jeremiah and Ezekiel told the truth for Zedekiah did see the King of Babylon at Ribbah but his eyes were put out before he arrived in Babylon so that, although he was carried (led) there, he never saw the city.

THE FIELD AT ANATHOTH

The word of the Lord came to Jeremiah saying that Hanameel, the son of Shallum, his uncle, would come to him asking the prophet to purchase the farm at Anathoth, for the right of redemption belonged to Jeremiah.

Under the law of the Lord an estate can never be alienated.* If, however, because of reverses or poverty, or for any other reason, a man wishes to dispose of his holdings, he must offer it to the next of kin. Even though he may have sold it to another, and the kinsman is absent at the time, upon his return the kinsman can claim the land at its value. This is called the right of the kinsman (Lev. 25:25).

THE TITLE DEEDS

Hanameel, the son of Jeremiah's uncle, came to the prophet in the court of the prison, and asked him if he would purchase the farm at Anathoth which was in the district of Benjamin. The prophet knew this was of the Lord so he agreed to buy the place and weighed out the money, seventeen shekels of silver. Jeremiah declared:

"Then I signed the deed and sealed it, and the witnesses witnessed it, and I counted out the money in their hearing. I then took the sealed Deed of Purchase, with its laws and conditions, and the deed of possession, and gave the Deed of Purchase to Baruk-ben-Nediah-ben-Maksiah in the presence of Hanamul [Hanameel] my

* See "Digest of the Divine Law," Chapter IX *Property Rights.* $3.00 postpaid. DESTINY Publishers, Merrimac, Mass. 01860

cousin, and in the presence of the witnesses who had signed the Deed of Purchase, in the presence of all the Jews detained in the courtyard, and instructed Baruk in their presence, saying: "Thus says the Lord of Hosts; the God of Israel, 'Take these deeds, this Deed of Purchase with its seals, and the Deed of Possession, and put them in an earthenware jar, so that they may be preserved for a long time ,'" (Jer. 32:10-14, *F. F. Trans.*)

Ferrar Fenton has the following footnote accompanying the above verses referring to this transaction:

"The reader should remember that in Jeremiah's day deeds and writings were made on stone, slates, or clay tablets, afterwards baked, and so not liable to decay as paper is."

The transaction completed, Jeremiah prophesied:

"Thus saith the Lord of hosts, the God of Israel; Houses and fields and vineyards shall be possessed again in this land." (Jer. 32:15.)

PURCHASE SIGNIFICANT

This notable transaction is recorded here for it has a prophetic significance and will yet contribute to the glory of God and to the identification of Israel and their right to the land of promise. These deeds, one sealed and one unsealed, were given by Jeremiah to Baruch, his scribe, for burial in an earthen vessel, the prophet expressly stating that in later generations the "heirs" (latter-day Israel) would recover them. These precautions taken by Jeremiah regarding the actuality and the legality of the transaction imply that these documents will one day bear witness in behalf of the rightful heirs to their legal right to the inheritance which was purchased by Jeremiah.

The transaction required the exercise of implicit faith in God on the part of Jeremiah. He was an old man and the enemy was already encamped on the very parcel of land he was to purchase. But recognizing the significance of this purchase as it would affect the future, Jeremiah prayed:

"Ah Lord God! behold, thou hast made the heaven and the earth by thy great power and stretched out arm, and there is nothing too hard for thee." (Jer. 32: 17.)

Humanly speaking, the transaction appeared to be a hopeless waste of time, for how could this land ever again be inhabited by God's people? Was it possible for peaceful transactions and commerce to be carried on again by His people in the land of Palestine? These were the questions troubling Jeremiah; yet God promised houses and that the land would be possessed again in this very place. In the face of the seemingly insurmountable obstacles, nevertheless, which made the situation apparently hopeless, the prophet recognized that nothing is too hard for God to perform and he acknowledged that none of God's promises would fail.

THE MIGHTY GOD

The prophet speaks of the loving-kindness of God and declares He will repay the iniquity of those who sin. He refers to the Lord as the Mighty God, affirms that

His name is the Lord of Hosts; that is, the Lord of Battles, and declares He is:

"Great in counsel, and mighty in work: for thine eyes are open upon all the ways of the sons of men: to give every one according to his ways, and according to the fruit of his doings." (Jer. 32: 19.)

SIGN AND A WITNESS

The prophet referred to certain signs and wonders in the land of Egypt which existed in his day:

"Which hath set signs and wonders in the land of Egypt, even unto this day." (Jer. 32: 20.)

What were those signs and wonders in the land of Egypt of which Jeremiah was speaking? Can it be that Jeremiah was fully aware of the significance of the Great Pyramid (as well as the Sphinx) which, according to Isaiah, would in the last days become a witness to His people:

"In that day shall there be an altar to the Lord in the midst of the land of Egypt, and a pillar at the border thereof to the Lord. And it shall be for a sign and for a witness unto the Lord of hosts in the land of Egypt." (Isa. 19: 19-20.)

Today, in the land of Egypt the two witnesses stand, the Great Pyramid and the Sphinx, which were evidently not only known to Isaiah but to Jeremiah as well. The facts concerning these witnesses are a separate story and an outline of that which is told by the Great Pyramid can be found in *The Challenge of the Great Pyramid**. This witness is the Bible in stone and substantiates

* 50 cents postpaid. DESTINY Publishers, Merrimac, Mass.

the story the Bible tells, giving interesting and significant chronological evidence concerning the times and seasons in which we live. The Sphinx is no less important and its story is revealed in part in *The Stars Declare God's Handiwork.**

A DISOBEDIENT PEOPLE

The prophet declares God brought His people out of the land of Egypt with signs and wonders and gave them the land which He had sworn to their fathers He would give to them, a land flowing with milk and honey. Though they had possessed this land for many years, Israel had failed to obey Him and walk in accordance with His laws. How could Jeremiah state that the people had done nothing at all which the Lord had commanded them when many individuals among them had obeyed God and kept His laws? He could make this declaration because the prophet was not referring to the individual but to *national* failure to observe and administer the law of the Lord as the law of the land. As a nation Israel had refused to do all this and Jeremiah condemned *the nation*, declaring that for this reason all the evil which they were experiencing had come upon them.

A QUESTIONING PROPHET

At the very time Jeremiah was speaking, the engines of war were casting their shots against the city and the earthen mounds were being raised to enable the assailants to shoot their arrows and throw their stones over

* 50 cents postpaid. DESTINY Publishers, Merrimac, Mass.

its walls. Jerusalem was being besieged by the Chaldeans when God commanded the prophet to purchase the farm and so he says:

"Here are the siege-mounds for storming the city, and under the sword, the famine, and the pestilence, the city is sure to fall into the hands of the Chaldean besiegers! Thy threat has been fulfilled, as thou seest. And it was thou, O Lord Eternal, who didst tell me to buy the land for money: I had the deeds written and sealed and witnessed, and here is the city falling into the hands of the Chaldeans!" (Jer. 32: 24-25 *Moffatt Trans.*)

Why should God command Jeremiah to buy a farm in a land that was about to be taken over by the enemy? This was a natural question for the prophet to ask. But the word of the Lord came to Jeremiah saying:

"Behold, I am the Lord, the God of all flesh: Is there anything too hard for me?" (Jer. 32: 27.)

GOD'S CHALLENGE

God thus challenges all those who question His ability to bring to pass all which He has spoken. Not only did the Lord confirm the fact that the city was to be captured by Nebuchadnezzar, King of Babylon, but He also stated that it would be burned with fire and all the houses destroyed. The reason given was because the people had offered incense to Baal upon the roofs of their houses and poured out drink-offerings to other Gods, dishonoring Jehovah, the God of Israel:

"For the children of Israel and the children of Judah

have only done evil before me from their youth [*i.e.*, from the time they had become a nation at Mount Sinai]: for the children of Israel have only provoked me to anger with the work of their hands, saith the Lord." (Jer. 32: 30.)

The Lord said of Jerusalem:

"For this city hath been to me as a provocation of mine anger and of my fury from the day that they built it even unto this day; that I should remove it from before my face, Because of all the evil of the children of Israel, and of the children of Judah, which they have done to provoke me to anger, they, their kings, their princes, their priests, and their prophets, and the men of Judah, and the inhabitants of Jerusalem." (Jer. 32: 31-32.)

Though the Lord declared He had taught His people the right way, yet they had turned their backs to Him and refused to pay any attention to His instructions. They would not listen or be subject to His corrections. The people had gone so far in their idolatrous worship that they had set up idols in the court of the Temple, thus indicating a hopelessly depraved spiritual condition.

THE BLESSINGS TO COME

Yet, though all the evil of which Jeremiah was speaking was to come upon his generation because of their sins, and the city itself was doomed to destruction, the Lord pointed to a time to come when He will surely bless His people:

"Behold, I will gather them out of all countries, whither I have driven them in mine anger, and in my fury, and in great wrath; and I will bring them again unto this place, and I will cause them to dwell safely: And they shall be my people, and I will be their God: And I will give them one heart, and one way, that they may fear me for ever, for the good of them, and of their children after them: And I will make an everlasting covenant with them, that I will not turn away from them, to do them good; but I will put my fear in their hearts, that they shall not depart from me." (Jer. 32: 37-40.)

DAY OF FULFILLMENT

Here is a description of God's people in the latter days under the terms and blessings of the New Covenant. Israel will have then turned to the Lord with all their hearts and will be serving Him and keeping His commandments, statutes and judgments. The Lord informed the Prophet that just as He had brought all the evil upon the people in Jeremiah's time, so will He bring good to them at a future time. In that day the prophecy that men will buy fields again in the land of Judea will be fulfilled:

"Men shall buy fields for money, and subscribe evidences, and seal them, and take witnesses in the land of Benjamin, and in the places about Jerusalem, and in the cities of Judah, and in the cities of the mountains, and in the cities of the valley, and in the cities of the south: for I will cause their captivity to return, saith the Lord." (Jer. 32: 44.)

Already in Palestine we are witnessing the beginning of the fulfillment of this promise, even though at present the land is afflicted with trouble. The House of Israel is now in possession of their ancient home land, though for the time being the turmoil and trouble caused by the national, but unscriptural, aspirations of the Jews is preventing the fullness of the realization of the blessings. But these blessings will yet be enjoyed to the full by Israel, following the complete settlement of the Jewish question. This will be made possible when His people awaken to their origin, identity and responsibility.

A CRITICAL TIME

Jeremiah was living in a most critical time, for the House of Israel had already been carried away into Assyrian captivity and the House of Judah was about to be taken away to Babylon. Also, insofar as a ruler of the line of David was concerned, there was to be no man sitting upon his throne ruling any more over the House of Judah in Jerusalem. The prophet could not help but be tremendously concerned for the future of the Kingdom and the House of David.

The word of the Lord came to Jeremiah while he was still in prison and His admonition to the prophet made it clear that He who is able to promise is also able to fulfill His promises. Jeremiah was told by the Lord to ask of Him and he would show him great events and reveal things to come.

This is a definite rebuke for all those theologians who

discount prophecy and refuse to believe the prophetic
declarations of the prophets concerning the future. Because of their unbelief God has sent them a strong delu-
sion and they believe a lie for, having failed to come to
Him who can reveal the future, the prophetic word is
a closed book and they are unable to understand it. But
the Spirit of God does reveal to men of God the marvelous fulfillment of coming events to which the prophets
referred:

"For the prophecy came not in old time by the will
of man: but holy men of God spake as they were moved
by the Holy Ghost." (II Peter 1: 21.)

REVEALING THINGS TO COME

Jeremiah was informed that the houses of Jerusalem
and the Royal palaces had been broken up that the
material might be used to build barricades against the
coming attack by the Chaldeans. He prophesied that
these places of defense would be filled with the corpses
of the slain of the city. God's favor had been withdrawn
because of the wickedness of the inhabitants of Jerusalem and they were to be given to the slaughter.

But God looks down the ages to the end of the period
of chastisement when both Israel and Judah will again
be restored to God's favor. At that time the wounds of
the city will be healed and God will give its citizens a
rich and enduring peace. Both Israel and Judah are to
be cleansed from the guilt of their sins against Jehovah
and Jerusalem will be known as a city of praise among
the nations who will be tremendously stirred by the

prosperity and peace God will confer upon Jerusalem. This will occur when the following has been completely fulfilled:

"For Zion's sake will I not hold my peace, and for Jerusalem's sake I will not rest, until the righteousness thereof go forth as brightness, and the salvation thereof as a lamp that burneth. And the Gentiles shall see thy righteousness, and all kings thy glory: and thou shalt be called by a new name, which the mouth of the Lord shall name." (Isa. 62: 1-2.)

It will be the day when the Kingdom of our Lord shall be established over all nations and:

"Many nations shall come, and say, Come, and let us go up to the mountain of the Lord, and to the house of the God of Jacob; and he will teach us of his ways, and we will walk in his paths: for the law shall go forth of Zion, and the word of the Lord from Jerusalem." (Micah 4: 2.)

Though Jeremiah was living in the midst of the siege of Jerusalem, and the city would soon be taken and the survivors of the siege led away captive, God encouraged the Prophet with the following prophecy regarding the future of His people and the city of Jerusalem:

"Thus saith the Lord: Again there shall be heard in this place, which ye say shall be desolate without man and without beast, even in the cities of Judah, and in the streets of Jerusalem, that are desolate, without man, and without inhabitant, and without beast, The voice of joy and the voice of gladness, the voice of the bridegroom, and the voice of the bride, the voice of them that shall say, Praise the Lord of hosts: for the Lord is good; for his mercy endureth for ever." (Jer. 33: 10-11.)

RESTORATION PROMISED

Continuing with this message of encouragement to Jeremiah the Lord promised that men will return to the land, cities will be built and inhabited, while shepherds will attend their flocks which will lie down in security in the fields of Palestine once more. This will be in the day when God carries out His gracious purposes concerning the House of Israel and the House of Judah. And so:

"In those days, and at that time, will I cause the Branch of righteousness to grow up unto David; and he shall execute judgment and righteousness in the land." (Jer. 33: 15.)

This looks forward to the coming of the Lord when He shall take over the Throne of His father David and reign over the House of Jacob for ever. Isaiah was prophesying of the wisdom and righteousness of His administration when he said:

"And the spirit of the Lord shall rest upon him, the spirit of wisdom and understanding, the spirit of counsel and might, the spirit of knowledge and of the fear of the Lord . . . With righteousness shall he judge the poor, and reprove with equity for the meek of the earth." (Isa. 11: 2 & 4.)

It must not be overlooked that from the very inception of the Kingdom at Mount Sinai it was destined to grow until a reign of peace under the benevolent rule of its King would be finally established throughout the earth. Thus Isaiah could prophesy:

"Of the increase of his government and peace there shall be no end, upon the throne of David, and upon his kingdom, to order it, and to establish it with judgment and with justice from henceforth even for ever. The zeal of the Lord of hosts will perform this." (Isa. 9: 7.)

DAVID'S POSTERITY

There is an important factor involved in this promise. Unless the Davidic throne is established in perpetuity and his kingdom continued without a break, this promise, made through the prophet Isaiah, could not possibly be fulfilled. Humanly speaking, the existence of the throne was about to cease as Jeremiah watched events and saw the Chaldeans building their mounds in preparation for the taking of Jerusalem. Zedekiah was to be taken captive and his sons slain. How, then, was the line of David to be continued that Isaiah's prophecy might be fulfilled? In this dark hour in the history of the House of David the Lord spoke to Jeremiah:

"For thus saith the Lord; David shall never want a man to sit upon the throne of the house of Israel." (Jer. 33: 17.)

Moffatt translates this:

"For this is the Eternal's promise: A Davidic king shall never be lacking to sit upon the throne of Israel."

Because of disbelief on the part of theologians and their ignorance of a law in Israel, church leaders have for the most part completely failed to recognize that with the death of the sons of Zedekiah the inheritance passed to a daughter who became the heir apparent to the Throne of David. This was in accordance with the following judgment rendered by God at the request of Moses in behalf of the daughters of Zelophehad:

"And thou shall speak unto the children of Israel, saying, If a man die, and have no son, then ye shall cause his inheritance to pass unto his daughter." (Num. 27: 8.)

ZEDEKIAH'S HEIR

With the death of Zedekiah's sons the inheritance of the Throne of David passed to his daughter under this law. The fact that the Lord declared the perpetuity of the Throne of David and its continuation over the House of Israel—not Judah—immediately raises a question. Where did Zedekiah's daughter go when she left Palestine? To what place did she eventually come where the Davidic rule could be continued uninterrupted, although over the House of Israel instead of the House of Judah? Later we shall follow the fortunes of Jeremiah as he journeyed to the *appointed place* where he was able to fulfill the latter half of his mission—to build and to plant. A large part of the planting had to do with establishing in perpetuity the House and Throne of David that David might never lack a man to reign over the House of Israel. For this reason the King's daughter became the special ward of the prophet.

A FALSE DEDUCTION

Theological commentators, failing to see the earthly continuity of the House of David ruling over the Kingdom, have declared that the promise God made to Jeremiah that David would never lack a man to rule upon the Throne of Israel is fulfilled in Jesus Christ who now sits upon the throne of the universe waiting until His enemies are made His footstool.

How illogical such a position can be becomes apparent to anyone who will give this question a little serious, *Biblical* consideration. Jesus Christ is not sitting upon a universal throne for He does not assume that royal position until He returns to take over the Throne in His Kingdom, at which time, according to the Angel in the annunciation to Mary, He will ascend the Throne of His father David and reign over the House of Jacob for ever. Men who say that over five hundred years after God spoke to Jeremiah the requirements of the prophecies were fulfilled in the birth of Jesus Christ, who never became king at that time, manifest, to say the least, a mind incapable of weighing evidence. And to add to all this the declaration that He is sitting upon a universal throne in fulfillment of these prophecies, which state definitely that the kings of David's line would sit upon a throne ruling over the *House of Israel*, shows to what lengths unreasoning theologians will go who do not believe the truth. The men of David's line are to sit upon the Throne of David which is to be established over the House of Israel according to the promise. This has reference to the continuity of the earthly Throne over the Kingdom with a man of the lineage of David sitting upon it.

THE PRIESTS, THE LEVITES

Along with that promise is the declaration:

"Neither shall the priests the Levites want a man before me to offer burn-offerings, and to kindle meat-offerings, and to do sacrifice continually." (Jer. 33: 18.)

Are these Levites also functioning in some far off universal kingdom? This is a legitimate question for the Levites were the administrators of the requirements of the law in the Kingdom and also waited upon the Throne to carry out the instructions of the King. They were the tax collectors, the doctors, lawyers and constituted all those who had charge of the affairs of state. If the King of the line of David is now upon a universal throne, the Levites must also be there ministering to His needs. This alone demonstrates the foolishness of the type of reasoning that tries to place Jesus Christ upon a throne that was to be occupied by earthly rulers of the line of David.

If Jeremiah had referred to the Aaronic Priesthood instead of the Levitical order he would have introduced confusion in the text, for the Aaronic order offered only temple sacrifices. The Levitical order rendered sacrificial service in the Kingdom. The burnt offerings and the meat offerings prepared by this order of priesthood had to do with preparing and inspecting the meat consumed as food by the people. Today this office is being carried out in the official inspection and governmental approval of the meat supplied to the people.

CERTAINTY OF THE COVENANT

God not only confirms the perpetuity of the Kingdom by referring to the ordinances of heaven but also to the continuity of the Davidic throne in the same way.

"Thus saith the Lord; If ye can break my covenant of the day, and my covenant of the night, and that there should not be day and night in their season: Then may also my covenant be broken with David my servant, that he should not have a son to reign upon his throne; and with the Levites the priests, my ministers. As the host of heaven cannot be numbered, neither the sand of the sea measured: so will I multiply the seed of David my servant, and the Levites that minister unto me." (Jer. 33: 20-22.)

ESTABLISHED IN PERPETUITY

If there were no other reason than this declaration on which to base our faith in the continued existence of the Throne of David, with a man somewhere upon the earth today reigning on that Throne over some portion of the House of Israel, this declaration by God to Jeremiah would be sufficient evidence to sustain our belief. The man of God will accept this confirmation of God's promise as a fact, knowing it to be true, and await the revelation of time which he knows will certainly substantiate his faith.

The original covenant God made with David was:

"And thine house and thy kingdom shall be established for ever before thee: thy throne shall be established for ever." (II Sam. 7: 16.)

God has promised three unconditional things to David:

1st) The continuity of David's House.

2nd) The endurance of his Kingdom.

3rd) The perpetuity of his Throne.

God confirmed the certainty of this covenant which he made with David as set forth in the Psalm:

"I have made a covenant with my chosen, I have sworn unto David my servant, Thy seed will I establish for ever, and build up thy throne to all generations . . . I have found David my servant; with my holy oil have I anointed him . . . My mercy will I keep for him for evermore, and my covenant shall stand fast with him. His seed also will I make to endure for ever, and his throne as the days of heaven. If his children forsake my law, and walk not in my judgments; If they break my statutes, and keep not my commandments; Then will I visit their transgression with the rod, and their iniquity with stripes. Nevertheless my lovingkindness will I not utterly take from him, nor suffer my faithfulness to fail. My covenant will I not break, nor alter the thing that is gone out of my lips. Once have I sworn by my holiness that I will not lie unto David. His seed shall endure for ever, and his throne as the sun before me. It shall be established for ever as the moon, and as a faithful witness in heaven." (Ps. 89: 3, 4, 20, 28-37.)

COVENANT WITH DAY AND NIGHT

Anyone who questions the continuity of David's House, Kingdom and Throne manifests a refusal to believe God and brings into question His sworn word and the surety of the fulfillment of His covenants. God establishes the reliability of His covenant with David through Jeremiah by referring to His covenant with day and night. That covenant was:

"While the earth remaineth, seedtime and harvest, and cold and heat, and summer and winter, and day and night shall not cease." (Gen. 8: 22.)

And so God declares:

"If ye can break my covenant of the day, and my covenant of the night, and that there should not be day and night in their season; Then may also my covenant be broken with David my servant, that he should not have a son to reign upon his throne; and with the Levites the priests, my ministers. As the host of heaven cannot be numbered, neither the sand of the sea measured: so will I multiply the seed of David my servant, and the Levites that minister unto me." (Jer. 33: 20-22.)

DISBELIEF CONDEMNED

The word of the Lord came to Jeremiah again and this time He condemned all those who in Jeremiah's day were declaring that God had cast off forever the two families (Israel and Judah) which He had chosen. This condemnation has a prophetic significance extending to the present time to include modern scholarship and that school of theological teaching which refuses to recognize the Scriptural teachings concerning the preservation of the House of Israel to this day, a people apart from the House of Judah or the Jews, and over whom reigns a man of the line of David. Because men refuse to recognize that the House of Israel is represented by nations in the world today, God declares they are despising His people. He confirms the certainty of fulfillment of His covenant in this crisis hour in the history of His people. The covenant is made with the seed of Abraham, Isaac and Jacob, and with His servant David, and He looks forward to the day of their deliverance from bondage:

"Thus saith the Lord; If my covenant be not with day and night, and if I have not appointed the ordinances of heaven and earth; Then will I cast away the seed of Jacob, and David my servant, so that I will not take any of his seed to be rulers over the seed of Abraham, Isaac, and Jacob: for I will cause their captivity to return, and have mercy on them." (Jer. 33: 25-26.)

Here we have a double witness to His promise that He will keep his covenant with David. The continuity of David's House, Kingdom and Throne are assured and today there is a man of the line of David ruling over the seed of Abraham, Isaac and Jacob in fulfillment of these promises. Only the blindness of unbelief on the part of the Christian world prevents many from seeing the truth and recognizing these great and wonderful facts which, when understood and believed, fully substantiate God's Word.

CHAPTER XIII

BURNING THE SACRED SCROLL

From the thirty-fourth chapter of Jeremiah to the end of his book we do not have a consecutive chronological record of events. Instead, recorded for our information is a summary of facts and incidents in the life of Jeremiah pertaining to the controversy he was having with those in authority. It is very likely that these prophecies are recorded in this way to emphasize the certainty of the statements of the Lord reiterated by Jeremiah to Zedekiah. Let us, therefore, continue to deal with the book of Jeremiah in the order in which its prophecies are given, at the same time taking careful note of their chronological setting.

PROPHECY CONCERNING ZEDEKIAH

Jeremiah had prophesied that the city of Jerusalem would be taken and Zedekiah would be led away captive. This was the word of the Lord which had come to the prophet at the time Nebuchadnezzar and his armies came against Jerusalem and the cities of Judah:

"Thus saith the Lord, the God of Israel, Go and speak to Zedekiah king of Judah, and tell him, Thus saith the Lord; Behold, I will give this city into the hand of the king of Babylon, and he shall burn it with fire: And thou shalt not escape out of his hand, but. shalt surely be taken, and delivered into his hand; and thine eyes shall behold the eyes of the king of Babylon, and he shall speak with thee mouth to mouth, and thou shalt go to Babylon." (Jer. 34: 2-3.)

Emphasis was placed upon Zedekiah's eyes and because Jeremiah declared he would see Nebuchadnezzar and be taken to Babylon, while Ezekiel had declared he would not see Babylon (Ez. 12: 13), Zedekiah believed neither of the prophets. This apparent discrepancy was further borne out in that Ezekiel declared the king would die in the land of the Chaldeans while Jeremiah prophesied he would not die by the sword, but would die in peace and at his death a peaceful funeral service would be held and the people would lament for him (Jer. 34: 5). All these prophecies came true, nevertheless, as verified by the record, for Zedekiah did not perish by the sword. He did meet and talk with Nebuchadnezzar, the King of Babylon, after which his eyes were put out and he was taken away to Babylon where he died in peace.

LIBERTY PROCLAIMED

In the stress and troubles afflicting Jerusalem Zedekiah made a covenant with the people at Jerusalem to proclaim liberty throughout the land. Every man should set free his man-servant, and maid-servant, if Hebrews, according to the requirements of the Law of Release. Under the Law of the Lord, when an Israelite had served six years for a debt, he was to go free in the seventh year.* It was in accordance with the require-

---

* See "Digest of the Divine Law," $3.00 postpaid. DESTINY Publishers, Merrimac, Mass. 01860

ments of this law that Zedekiah called for the liberation of the people.

After this proclamation had been issued, and men and women were set free, the princes and people changed their minds, turned from the law, and forced the servants and handmaids, whom they had set free, into bondage again. The word of the Lord came to Jeremiah saying:

"Thus saith the Lord, the God of Israel; I made a covenant with your fathers in the day that I brought them forth out of the land of Egypt, out of the house of bondmen, saying, At the end of seven years let ye go every man his brother an Hebrew, which hath been sold [who had sold himself] unto thee; and when he hath served thee six years, thou shalt let him go free from thee: but your fathers hearkened not unto me, neither inclined their ear. And ye were now turned, and had done right in my sight, in proclaiming liberty every man to his neighbour, and ye had made a covenant before me in the house which is called by my name: But ye turned and polluted my name, and caused every man his servant, and every man his handmaid, whom he had set at liberty at their pleasure, to return, and brought them into subjection, to be unto you for servants and for handmaids." (Jer. 34: 13-16.)

REPUDIATING THE COVENANT

It is evident that, due to the fact that Pharaoh's army was advancing from Egypt, the Babylonians withdrew from the siege of the city (see verses 21 & 22).

Because of the seriousness of the situation before the armies withdrew, Zedekiah had made the proclamation to liberate all who were enslaved, and the men and women had been set free. When the danger from the armies of Nebuchadnezzar seemed to pass, the princes and people, who had set the slaves free, seized them again, pressing them back into service. This proclamation had been issued in the name of the Lord. The calf had been slain, solemnizing the covenant, for the princes of Judah and Jerusalem, with the officials, officers and priests, and the people, had passed between the sacrificial parts of the slain animal. This act, in the name of the Lord, signified that, as the sacrificial animal was cut in two, so would they be subject to be cut in twain if they broke their covenant. The Lord declared:

"Ye have not hearkened unto me, in proclaiming liberty, every one to his brother, and every man to his neighbour: behold, I proclaim a liberty for you, saith the Lord, to the sword, to the pestilence, and to the famine; and I will make you to be removed into all the kingdoms of the earth. I will give the men that have transgressed my covenant, which have not performed the words of the covenant which they had made before me, when they cut the calf in twain, and passed between the parts thereof . . . I will even give them into the hand of their enemies, and into the hand of them that seek their life: and their dead bodies shall be for meat unto the fowls of the heaven, and to the beasts of the earth." (Jer. 34: 17-20.)

CHALDEANS TO RETURN

Having pronounced judgment upon the people for their hypocrisy in refusing to keep the Law of Release after they had taken a solemn oath to do so, God declared the army of Nebuchadnezzar had only withdrawn from the siege of the city in order to meet the threat from Egypt:

"And Zedekiah king of Judah and his princes will I give into the hand of their enemies, and into the hand of them that seek their life, and into the hand of the king of Babylon's army, which are gone up from you. Behold, I will command, saith the Lord, and cause them to return to this city; and they shall fight against it, and take it, and burn it with fire: and I will make the cities of Judah a desolation without an inhabitant." (Jer. 34: 21-22.)

IMPORTANCE OF OATH

Many overlook the fact that God requires His people to obey *all* His laws. Every vow taken must be fulilled. Zedekiah, the King, with his princes and all the people, had taken a vow and made an oath that they would keep the provisions of the economic Law of Release, then deliberately refused to keep their vow. The result of their broken vow is set forth in the judgment God pronounced against them when He numbered them for slaughter for refusing to keep the covenant and oath they had taken. Their sin would not have been so great if they had not made a solemn vow to let the people go free and then repudiated their oath. Solomon said:

"When thou vowest a vow unto God, defer not to pay it; for he hath no pleasure in fools: pay that which thou hast vowed. Better is it that thou shouldest not vow, than that thou shouldest vow and not pay." (Ecc. 5:4-5.)

Under the law:

"When thou shalt vow a vow unto the Lord thy God, thou shalt not slack to pay it: for the Lord thy God will surely require it of thee; and it would be sin in thee." (Deut. 23:21.)

It is very evident that God allowed the army of Nebuchadnezzar to withdraw so that He might test His people to see if they had truly experienced a change of heart. But Zedekiah and the people failed the test. They had taken a solemn oath in a time of great national danger and, when the danger seemed to have passed, they immediately proceeded to ignore the provisions of the covenant they had made with God. In this account we have a clear demonstration of God's attitude toward all who refuse to keep their solemn vows which many today often make in the face of a crisis and proceed to forget after the crisis has passed.

THE SONS OF JONADAB

The prophecies and events related in the thirty-fifth and thirty-sixth chapters of Jeremiah belong in the reign of Jehoiakim and are evidently recorded at this time, following the predictions concerning Zedekiah and the judgments that were about to descend upon Jerusalem, to give force to the prophecies Jeremiah was uttering against Zedekiah.

Reference is made to the instruction God gave to Jeremiah in the days of Jehoiakim asking him to go to the family of the Rechabites, invite them into one of the chambers of the Temple and place wine before them to drink. The prophet did as he was bidden:

"But they said, We will drink no wine: for Jonadab the son of Rechab our father commanded us, saying, Ye shall drink no wine, neither ye, nor your sons for ever: Neither shall ye build house, nor sow seed, nor plant vineyard, nor have any: but all your days ye shall dwell in tents; that ye may live many days in the land where ye be strangers." (Jer. 35:6-7.)

Jeremiah was informed that this word had been kept by them and by their wives, sons and daughters. However, when Nebuchadnezzar came against Palestine they had entered the city of Jerusalem for fear of the armies of the Chaldeans and Syrians.

JUDAH'S LACK OF OBEDIENCE

The fidelity of this family to their father's instructions is used of the Lord who commanded Jeremiah to tell the men of Judah and the inhabitants of Jerusalem:

"Will ye not receive instruction to hearken to my words? saith the Lord. The words of Jonadab the son of Rechab, that he commanded his sons not to drink wine, are performed; for unto this day they drink none, but obey their father's commandment: notwithstanding

I have spoken unto you, rising early and speaking; but ye hearkened not unto me." (Jer. 35: 13-14.)

The expression "rising early" is used in connection with the Lord's instructions through His prophets and implies that He always warns far enough in advance of punishment to urge every man to turn from his evil course and mend his ways. The warning had been repeatedly given, calling them to turn from idolatry that God might bring a blessing upon them but they would not listen. God shows the contrast between the obedience of the sons of Jonadab and the lack of such obedience on the part of His people, and He says:

"Therefore thus saith the Lord God of hosts, the God of Israel; Behold, I will bring upon Judah, and upon all the inhabitants of Jerusalem all the evil that I have pronounced against them: because I have spoken unto them, but they have not heard; and I have called unto them, but they have not answered." (Jer. 35: 17.)

THE RECHABITES BLESSED

A blessing was pronounced upon the family of the Rechabites because they were obedient to the commands of their father:

"Therefore thus saith the Lord of hosts, the God of Israel; Jonadab the son of Rechab shall not want [never lack] a man to stand before me for ever." (Jer. 35: 19.)

This incident relating to the house of Jonadab was evidently recited by Jeremiah before the inhabitants of Jerusalem and the King of Judah as a reminder to them of their continued disobedience since the days of Jehoiakim. But the prophet also demonstrated God's mercy toward those who obey Him.

JEREMIAH INSTRUCTED TO WRITE

The prophet next records another incident which transpired in the fourth year of the reign of Jehoiakim. Having demonstrated the refusal of the people and the King to obey God's commands, Jeremiah demonstrated their attitude toward the words of the Lord in the action of Jehoiakim who burned the records of Jeremiah's prophecies. The word of the Lord had come to Jeremiah in the fourth year of the reign of Jehoiakim saying:

"Take thee a roll of a book, and write therein all the words that I have spoken unto thee against Israel, and against Judah, and against all the nations, from the day I have spake unto thee, from the days of Josiah, even unto this day." (Jer. 36: 2.)

IMPORTANCE OF WRITTEN WORD

Why did God instruct the prophet to commit His words to writing? Because of the importance of the message, it was necessary to do so or it would soon be forgotten. What do we know today of the thousands of words spoken but not recorded by the prophets and apostles as they served the people of their day? Nothing whatever, for, apart from what was committed to writing, there is no way to recall to remembrance the many things which were said.

Platform work has its place, but the spoken word at

its best is like a comet that suddenly flares as a brilliant spectacle flashing across the evening sky and then disappears, passing out into infinite space, never again to be seen by man. But the written word is as the light of the sun shining day after day. It not only provides illumination for those who are living but will continue to exist to enlighten multitudes as yet unborn who will read and understand because of the continued shining light of revelation preserved in the written word.

The messages God gave to Jeremiah were so important He required the prophet to commit them to writing. This presupposes the need of passing the records along to later generations for only thus could the utterances of the prophet be preserved. Then, too, by committing all his prophecies to writing it would serve as a continuous warning, not only to his generation, but to generations to come, of the ultimate end of a people choosing to pursue an evil course. Furthermore, the written word would go, even in his day, where the spoken word would never be heard. In this particular instance Jeremiah was in hiding and it would not have been safe for him to have appeared personally before the King, who sought his life as subsequent events clearly prove. Jeremiah, as a result of God's instruction, proceeded to write down all his prophecies and because he was able in that way to send word to the King, the Lord said:

"It may be that the house of Judah will hear all the evil which I purpose to do unto them, that they may return every man from his evil way; that I may forgive their iniquity and their sin." (Jer. 36: 3.)

BARUCH READS THE BOOK

Jeremiah called Baruch, his scribe, and dictated all the words of the Lord to him, and Baruch wrote them down in the book; that is, upon the scroll. The prophet explained to Baruch that as he was shut up (not in prison, but in hiding) and could not go in person to the House of the Lord, Baruch was to go there on the next fast day and read the scroll in the hearing of the people. Jeremiah told his scribe that it might cause the people to turn from their evil ways. Baruch waited for the fast day which was proclaimed in the fifth year of the reign of Jehoiakim. All the people of Jerusalem and of the cities in Judah came to the Temple in Jerusalem:

"Then read Baruch in the book the words of Jeremiah in the house of the Lord . . . in the ears of all the people." (Jer. 36: 10.)

While Baruch was reading the scroll, it was reported to the princes of Judah. The princes took Baruch and brought him before their group and commanded that he read the book in their hearing:

"Now it came pass, when they had heard all the words, they were afraid both one and other, and said unto Baruch, We will surely tell the king of all these words." (Jer. 36: 16.)

BOOK READ BEFORE KING

Jeremiah had been warning of coming disaster for

many years. However, it was not until his words had been committed to writing that the princes, upon hearing those words read, began to realize the seriousness of their position. The princes, knowing that the life of both Jeremiah and Baruch might be in danger when the King heard the statements made in the book, counseled Baruch to go and hide himself with Jeremiah. For Baruch had informed them Jeremiah had dictated the prophecies to him and he had written them down in the book with ink.

The princes went before the King in the court and told him of the happening. This book, or roll, had already been given by the princes to Elishama, a scribe, and the King sent Jehudi to Elishama to secure the roll. Jehudi then read from the book in the presence of the King. The King was in his winter house with a fire burning on the hearth (a chafing dish or brazier in which a fire was burning) before him.

When Jehudi had read three or four leaves the king slashed them off the roll with a penknife and flung them into the fire burning upon the brazier in front of him. He continued to do this until the entire scroll was consumed. The record states of those present:

"Yet they were not afraid, nor rent their garments, neither the king, nor any of his servants that heard all these words." (Jer. 36: 24.)

DESTROYING THE WORD

All these men were so hardened in unbelief that this attack upon God's words made no impression upon them. This kind of attack upon the Word of God is duplicated today in modern unbelief as the ecclesiastical leaders and scholars question the accuracy of the Bible. The same tactics practiced by Jehoiakim are in evidence and the destruction of the authority of the Book is being as effectively accomplished as if it were consigned to the fire. When the modernists finish their criticism, about all that is left of the Bible are its covers. When Jehoiakim had completed his work upon the scroll, all he had left were the sticks upon which the scroll had been rolled. Jehoiakim used a penknife to mutilate the word of the Lord while the modernist uses his boasted worldly scholarship as his instrument of mutilation. The higher critic and modernist of today are as unafraid of their acts of vandalism in mutilating the Word of God as Jehoiakim and his princes were.

PROPHET AND SCRIBE ORDERED SEIZED

Elnathan, Delaiah and Gemariah made intercession with the King not to destroy the roll but he would not listen to them. Instead, he issued orders that Baruch and Jeremiah be seized, but their hiding place was not revealed for God was protecting them. This has always been the attitude of evil men against those whom God has used to convey warnings to them. A classic example of considering the messenger of the Lord one's enemy was the attitude of Ahab, King of Israel, toward Elijah, the prophet. Ahab had taken possession of Naboth's vineyard and God sent the prophet to the King to rebuke him for this evil and render judgment for his sin:

"And Ahab said to Elijah, Hast thou found me, O mine enemy? And he answered, I have found thee: because thou hast sold thyself to work evil in the sight of the Lord." (I Kings 21: 20.)

A SECOND BOOK PREPARED

Jeremiah was commanded to write upon a second roll, duplicating all that he had written upon the first. He was to send the following message to Jehoiakim:

"Thou hast burned the roll, saying, Why hast thou written therein, saying, The king of Babylon shall certainly come and destroy this land, and shall cause to cease from thence man and beast? Therefore thus saith the Lord of Jehoiakim king of Judah; He shall have none to sit upon the throne of David: and his dead body shall be cast out in the day to the heat, and in the night to the frost. And I will punish him and his seed and his servants for their iniquity; and I will bring upon them, and upon the inhabitants of Jerusalem, and upon the men of Judah, all the evil that I have pronounced against them; but they hearkened not." (Jer. 36: 29-31.)

JEHOIAKIM AND JEHOIACHIN

Jehoiakim, King of Judah, the son of Josiah, was the father of Jehoiachin, afterwards called Coniah, who was carried away to Babylon. The curse pronounced upon him here is the curse spoken of earlier by Jeremiah when he prophesied:

"He shall be buried with the burial of an ass, drawn

and cast forth beyond the gates of Jerusalem." (Jer. 22: 19.)

The reference to this judgment should have been very effective, for all the inhabitants of Jerusalem knew the fate of Jehoiakim when Nebuchadnezzar ordered his body thrown before the walls of Jerusalem where it lay without burial. Jehoiachin, or Coniah as Jeremiah refers to him, the son of Jehoiakim, was carried away captive to Babylon.

MULTILATORS OF SCRIPTURE

The severity of the judgment pronounced upon Jehoiakim for destroying God's word should cause those who are practicing the sin of this king in their multilation of the Bible to know that He will hold them personally responsible for so great a sin. Great as the sin of refusal to heed God's injunction is, the multilation of His Written Word is always the prelude to judgment. The present activities of modernist multilators will bring about its judgment, for men cannot escape the condemnation pronounced upon those who add to or take from His revelation.

Following the destruction of the first book, Jeremiah took another and gave it to Baruch, his scribe, who wrote as the prophet dictated all the words which were in the book destroyed by Jehoiakim. This second book included prophecies which had not been written in the first scroll.

CHAPTER XIV

THE DESTRUCTION OF JERUSALEM

Following the prophet's reference to the events which transpired during the reign of Jehoiakim, including the burning of the Book of his prophecies, Jeremiah next gave his experiences up to and including the capture of the city by Nebuchadnezzar, with a detailed account of the events which immediately followed the capitulation.

JEREMIAH WARNS ZEDEKIAH

Zedekiah, the son of Josiah, reigned at Jerusalem instead of Jehoiachin, or Coniah, whom Nebuchadnezzar had carried away to Babylon. But neither Zedekiah, his servants nor the people would listen to the word of the Lord communicated to them through Jeremiah. The King sent two messengers to Jeremiah, asking the prophet to pray to the Lord for him and for his people. This was while Jeremiah was at liberty to come and go as he pleased before he was thrown into jail.

Pharaoh's army had advanced from Egypt, compelling the Chaldeans to withdraw from the siege of Jerusalem, at which time the word of the Lord came to Jeremiah saying:

"Thus shall ye say to the king of Judah, that sent you unto me to enquire of me; Behold, Pharaoh's army, which is come forth to help you, shall return to Egypt into their own land. And the Chaldeans shall come again, and fight against this city, and take it, and burn

it with fire. Thus saith the Lord; Deceive not yourselves, saying, The Chaldeans shall surely depart from
us: for they shall not depart. For though ye had smitten
the whole army of the Chaldeans that fight against you,
and there remained but wounded men among them, yet
should they rise up every man in his tent, and burn this
city with fire." (Jer. 37: 7-10.)

EGYPTIAN'S NO HELP

Pharaoh's army would be of no help to Judah against
the Babylonians. Ridpath in his *History of the World*,
Vol. I, states:

"For some reason these people [the Jews] had come
to prefer Egyptian to Babylonian masters. Perhaps they
even hoped ultimately to throw off all mastery and become independent, as in the days of David. At any rate,
Zedekiah, after having kept his faith with Nebuchadnezzar for eight years, became at heart disloyal, and
entered into an intrigue with Egypt against the Babylonians.

"Pharaoh Apries was now the Egyptian ruler, a youth
whose ambition overleaped his prudence. He and Zedekiah took counsel together against the mighty, and it
was agreed that the Jewish king should revolt and that
the Egyptian should come to his support. Accordingly,
in B.C. 588, Zedekiah threw off his allegiance and gathered an army for defense. This was the fourth insurrec-
tion which had occurred since Palestine became a Babylonian dependency. Nebuchadnezzar was enraged. He
marched with his host against the city of the Jews, deso-

lating the country as he came. Jerusalem was at once
invested. Mounds were built against the walls, and the
place was already reduced to straits when Apries came
up from Egypt to succor his friend. Nebuchadnezzar,
for the time, gave up the siege, turned upon the Egyptians, whom he routed in battle and drove precipitately
into their own country. Zedekiah was thus left to his
fate."

THE PROPHET ARRESTED

After the temporary withdrawal of the Babylonian
army from the siege of Jerusalem to enable Nebuchadnezzar to meet the threat of Pharaoh's army, Jeremiah started to leave the city to go into the land of
Benjamin to take over some property among his own
people. Just as he reached the Benjamin-Gate of the
city he was arrested and accused of planning to desert
to the Babylonians. The prophet denied this but the
sentry arrested him and took him to the authorities. The
Princes were angered at the prophet and had him
flogged and thrown into prison where he was detained
for a long time. The place of his imprisonment seems
to have been the arched vaults under the house of
Jonathan, the scribe.

It is clearly evident from the record that Zedekiah
was afraid of the Princes who evidently were in charge
of the city's defenses. Because of his fear, the King sent
privately for Jeremiah and had an interview with him
in the Palace. The King desired to know if there was
any message from the Lord and Jeremiah said there
was:

"Thou shalt be delivered into the hand of the king of Babylon." (Jer. 37: 17.)

Jeremiah asked the King in what way he had offended him, his servants or the people that he should be confined in a prison. Evidently Nebuchadnezzar had returned by this time to again besiege Jerusalem, having defeated the Egyptian army. Zedekiah was very much concerned because Jeremiah's prediction was fulfilled. On the strength of this fulfillment Jeremiah asked Zedekiah:

"Pray where have you put your prophets, who assured you that the king of Babylon would never attack you or this country?" (Jer. 37: 19, *Moffatt Trans.*)

JEREMIAH'S PLEA

Because Jeremiah had told the truth, he was thoroughly disliked and had been unjustly thrown into prison. It was only natural that he should ask the King why he had failed to deal severely with the false prophets to whom he had listened, now that their predictions proved to be untrue. He used this occasion to plead his cause:

"Therefore hear now, I pray thee, O my Lord the king: let my supplication, I pray thee, be accepted before thee; that thou cause me not to return to the house of Jonathan the scribe, lest I die there." (Jer. 37: 20.)

It is very clear from the prophet's plea that the jailer was far from kind to him. In the East, and in those times, the jailer had absolute control over those in his charge and could allow them some freedom with good food, or he could be very oppressive and give scant and unwholesome food to those under his charge. Jeremiah's endurance under harsh treatment was coming to an end and he asked the King for relief.

"Then Zedekiah the king commanded that they should commit Jeremiah into the court of the prison, and that they should give him daily a piece of bread out of the bakers' street, until all the bread in the city were spent. Thus Jeremiah remained in the court of the prison." (Jer. 37: 21.)

COUNSEL TO SURRENDER

Food in Jerusalem was becoming very scarce as the result of the Babylonian siege of the city. The battle was being pressed by the Chaldeans and the Princes heard the message Jeremiah had given to all the people, saying:

"Thus saith the Lord, He that remaineth in this city shall die by the sword, by the famine, and by the pestilence: but he that goeth forth to the Chaldeans shall live; for he shall have his life for a prey, and shall live. Thus saith the Lord, This city shall surely be given into the hand of the king of Babylon's army, which shall take it." (Jer. 38: 2-3.)

Such utterances by Jeremiah were considered treasonable even though they were spoken in the name of the Lord, the God of Israel. Because of unbelief and a disregard for the law of God, Judah had reached the place when the predicted disaster for disobedience had come upon them. It was too late to prevent the destruction of the city, made inevitable by their rebellion against God, so the Lord, through His prophet Jeremiah, gave counsel to all those who would heed His words that they might escape the coming destruction.

TRUE PATRIOTISM

Patriotism means much more than to blindly support the policies of a government in opposition to God and to His laws. A true patriot is one who, for the love of his country, may find himself in opposition to political forces which have gained control and have the power and authority to act contrary to the ultimate welfare of the country. Jeremiah stood in the position of one who loved his people and his country, yet compelled to oppose the Princes, rulers and the people because of their unrighteousness. Because the nation had turned away from God and His law, the prophet had no alternative than to speak as he did. Therefore, the Princes said to the King:

"We beseech thee, let this man be put to death: for thus he weakeneth the hands of the men of war that remain in this city, and the hands of all the people, in speaking such words unto them: for this man seeketh not the welfare [peace] of this people, but the hurt." (Jer. 38: 4.)

It appears that these Princes were in complete control of the nation in this crisis, with power to act contrary to the ultimate good of all. Jeremiah, in following God's instructions, was compelled to oppose them for there was to be no peace in his generation. His patriotism, however, gave him a vision of a day that would come when real peace would be the blessing of those unborn generations who, in the far-off future, would heed God's instructions and accept the righteousness of His law.

THE PROPHET CAST INTO WELL

Zedekiah, the King, was powerless to act contrary to the wishes of his Princes so he said:

"Behold, he is in your hand . . . Then took they Jeremiah, and cast him into the dungeon . . . And in the dungeon there was no water, but mire; so Jeremiah sunk in the mire." (Jer. 38: 5-6.)

Actually, Jeremiah was cast into a deep well or cistern and, if left there, would certainly have perished. However, God called upon Ebed-melech, the Ethiopian, who was a eunuch in the King's house, and he appealed to the King in behalf of Jeremiah saying:

"My lord the king, these men have done evil in all that they have done to Jeremiah the prophet, whom they have cast into the dungeon; and he is like to die for hunger in the place where he is: for there is no more bread in the city." (Jer. 38: 9.)

The King commanded that the Ethiopian take men and ropes and pull Jeremiah out of the cistern before he died. The ropes were lowered with some torn and tattered rags which the prophet put under his arms so the ropes would not injure him and he was pulled out of the mire and up to the surface. Thereafter, the prophet stayed in the court of the prison.

KING SENDS FOR JEREMIAH

Zedekiah again sent for Jeremiah, telling him he would ask a question and the prophet was not to withhold anything. Jeremiah said:

"But if I tell you the truth, you will certainly put me to death, will you not? Besides you will not listen to any advice from me." (Jer. 38:15, *Moffatt Trans.*)

The King took an oath that he would not harm the prophet nor turn him over to the men who sought his life. Jeremiah then advised the King to surrender to Nebuchadnezzar, King of Babylon, and his life would be saved and the city spared from destruction. But the King told the prophet he was afraid that the Chaldeans might hand him over to the Jews who had deserted and they would ill-treat him.

Jeremiah assured the King this would not happen for the message he spoke was from the Lord and it would be well with him if he obeyed. If he refused to obey, however, it would be said by the women of the Palace when they were led away captive that Zedekiah's friends had encouraged him to 'oppose the Chaldeans against his better judgment. His family also would be taken and he would be the cause of the city being destroyed.

The conversation which followed between Jeremiah and Zedekiah indicates how the Princes dominated the King, for Zedekiah asked Jeremiah to keep what had passed between them secret and his life would be safe. If the Princes should ask him about the interview, the prophet was to tell them that he petitioned the King not to send him back to die at Jonathan's house. As the King had anticipated, the Princes did ask Jeremiah what had been said between him and the King and the prophet answered as the King had instructed him. Thus, the conversation that took place was not discovered and Jeremiah remained in the court of the prison until Jerusalem was taken, for he was there when the city fell.

FALL OF JERUSALEM

The account of the siege and fall of Jerusalem is given as follows:

"In the ninth year of Zedekiah king of Judah, in the tenth month, came Nebuchadnezzar king of Babylon and all his army against Jerusalem, and they besieged it. And in the eleventh year of Zedekiah, in the fourth month, the ninth day of the month, the city was broken up." (Jer. 39: 1-2.)

When Zedekiah and the garrison saw that the Babylonians had made a breach in the wall they took flight, leaving the city by night to seek security in the Jordan valley. But the Chaldeans pursued and overtook them near Jericho and Zedekiah was brought back to face Nebuchadnezzar, who was at Riblah.

All the nobles of Judah were slain, together with the sons of Zedekiah, and Zedekiah's eyes were put out. He was bound in chains and taken to Babylon. The King's house, as well as many of the homes of the people in Jerusalem, was burned, while the walls of the city were broken down. Nebuzar-adan, the Captain of the guard, carried away captive into Babylon all who had adhered to the Princes in their rebellion, leaving only the poor of the people in the land. These were allotted vineyards and fields.

INSTRUCTIONS REGARDING JEREMIAH

As for Jeremiah, Nebuchadnezzar had issued an order to the Captain of the guard:

"Take him, and look well to him, and do him no harm; but do unto him even as he shall say unto thee." (Jer. 39: 12.)

It has already been shown that Jeremiah in Jerusalem and Daniel in Babylon were close friends, and that Jeremiah had visited Daniel in Babylon. At that time Daniel, who was high in the court of Babylon, no doubt presented his friend to Nebuchadnezzar, the King. As time passed, the King of Babylon evidently became well acquainted with the work of Jeremiah and knew of his advice to Zedekiah. He was led of God to protect him and so issued the above orders to the head of his army. The prophet was taken out of prison and allowed to return to his home and remain among the people.

PROMISE TO THE ETHIOPIANS

While in prison the word of the Lord came to Jeremiah, telling him to speak to Ebed-Melech, the Ethiopian, and say that he was to be delivered and would not perish when the city fell because he had trusted in the Lord.

CAPTAIN AND KING'S TESTIMONY

The testimony of the Babylonian Captain of the

guard at the time he took Jeremiah from prison and removed the chains from him was as follows:

"The Lord thy God hath pronounced this evil upon this place. Now the Lord hath brought it, and done according as he hath said: because ye have sinned against the Lord, and have not obeyed his voice, therefore this thing is come upon you. And now, behold, I loose thee this day from the chains which were upon thine hand. If it seem good unto thee to come with me into Babylon, come; and I will look well unto thee: but if it seem ill unto thee to come with me into Babylon, forbear: behold, all the land is before thee: whither it seemeth good and convenient for thee to go, thither go." (Jer. 40: 2-4.)

This testimony is most interesting, for it clearly indicates that the Captain of the hosts of Babylon believed in the Lord. God had seen to it that a man who had charge of all the prisoners was a man who feared Him. We know that as a result of Daniel's activities in Babylon Nebuchadnezzar himself became a believer in the God of Israel. After he was restored to health, following his seven years of insanity, he testified:

"And at the end of the days I Nebuchadnezzar lifted up mine eyes unto heaven, and mine understanding returned unto me, and I blessed the most High; and I praised and honoured him that liveth for ever, whose dominion is an everlasting dominion, and his kingdom is from generation to generation: And all the inhabitants of the earth are reputed as nothing: And he doeth according to his will in the army of heaven, and among the inhabitants of the earth: and none can stay his hand, or say unto him, What doest thou? At the same time my reason returned unto me; and for the glory of my kingdom, mine honour and brightness returned unto me; and my counsellors and my lords sought unto me; and I was established in my kingdom, and excellent majesty was added unto me. Now I Nebuchadnezzar praise and extol and honour the King of heaven, all whose works are truth, and his ways judgment: and those that walk in pride he is able to abase." (Dan. 4: 34-37.)

Nebuchadnezzar's speech is a testimony to the influence of Daniel whom he declared had the Spirit of God upon his life. That influence was not confined to the King alone for, occupying a position of authority in Babylon, many must have come under Daniel's influence. It is very likely that the Captain of the guard, who was in charge of the forces of Babylon in the campaign against Judah and Jerusalem, became a believer in the God of Israel as a result of his contacts with Daniel at the court of Babylon.

ISHMAEL'S PLOT

Jeremiah went to Gedaliah, whom Nebuchadnezzar had made Governor over the cities of Judah. He was residing at Mizpah and with him were many of the people who were left in the land. After the Babylonian army had departed many fugitives gathered around Gedaliah and among them came a man by the name of Ishmael who intended to usurp the sceptre. His plot to kill Gedaliah was exposed by Johanan who informed

Gedaliah of the plan to slay him. Gedaliah, however, would not believe that Ishmael had any such intentions and reprimanded Johanan for desiring to slay Ishmael before the murder could be consummated. Johanan had informed the Governor that if Ishmael succeeded in carrying out his plans it would mean the dispersal of all the Jews which had rallied around him, bringing ruin upon all who were left in Judah. Instead of taking warning, Gedaliah informed Johanan that what he said about Ishmael was not true.

Ishmael, nevertheless, carried out his plot and slew Gedaliah and all the Jews who were with him. The next day, before anyone knew what had taken place, eighty pilgrims came with offerings for the Temple and Ishmael slew all but ten of them.

As soon as Johanan and the rest of the leaders of the Jewish forces heard of the crimes committed by Ishmael, who had carried off all the rest of the people of Mizpah as prisoners, together with the King's daughters, they pursued him and rescued the people. But Ishmael, with eight men, escaped and went over to the Ammonites.

Johanan and the people with him travelled on and stopped near Bethlehem, but with the intention of moving on to Egypt, for they were in fear of the Chaldeans because of what Ishmael had done in assassinating Gedaliah, whom the King of Babylon had appointed Governor over Judah.

CHAPTER XV

JEREMIAH TAKEN TO EGYPT

The Captains of the Jews' forces, together with Johanan and the people who were with them, came to Jeremiah with the plea:

"Let, we beseech thee, our supplication be accepted before thee, and pray for us unto the Lord thy God, even for all this remnant; (for we are left but a few of many, as thine eyes do behold us;) That the Lord thy God may shew us the way wherein we may walk, and the thing that we may do." (Jer. 42: 2-3.)

This seemed like a sincere request for guidance but, unfortunately, these people were seeking advice to confirm the program which they had already settled upon, for their minds were clearly made up to go to Egypt.

Jeremiah said he had heard their supplication and would pray about it to the Lord. Whatever the Lord showed him, he would in turn communicate to them. They replied:

"The Lord be a true and faithful witness between us; if we do not even according to all things for the which the Lord thy God shall send thee to us. Whether it be good, or whether it be evil, we will obey the voice of the Lord our God, to whom we send thee; that it may be well with us, when we obey the voice of the Lord our God." (Jer. 42: 5-6.)

THE MESSAGE OF THE LORD

This hypocritical show of willingness to follow the Lord, when in their hearts they had already determined upon the course of action they intended to pursue, condemned them before they had the answer from the Lord. Ten days after they petitioned Jeremiah he summoned Johanan and the leaders of the Jews, with the people, to hear the Lord's words. The prophet informed them they were to abide in the land and not go down into Egypt. He said they need not be afraid of the king of Babylon for God would deliver them from his hands and show mercy upon them.

Jeremiah then warned them that if they did not obey the voice of the Lord, but were determined to go to Egypt to dwell, thus hoping to see no more war or hear the sound of the trumpet or be hungry for bread:

"Then it shall come to pass, that the sword, which ye feared, shall overtake you there in the land of Egypt, and the famine, whereof ye were afraid, shall follow close after you there in Egypt; and there ye shall die. So shall it be with all the men that set their faces to go into Egypt, to sojourn there; they shall die by the sword, by the famine, and by the pestilence: and none of them shall remain or escape from the evil that I will bring upon them." (Jer. 42: 16-17.)

Just as God's anger and fury had been poured out on Jerusalem so, too, the prophet declared it would be poured out upon all those who went down to Egypt. They would become an execration and an astonishment, a curse and a reproach and would never again see the land of Judah. Jeremiah accused them of deluding themselves by asking him to pray to the Lord their God for guidance when they had already made up their minds concerning what they intended to do:

"Now therefore know certainly that ye shall die by the sword, by the famine, and by the pestilence, in the place whither ye desire to go and to sojourn." (Jer. 42: 22.)

THE LEADERS REBEL

When Jeremiah had finished telling the leaders and the people what the Lord had said they called the prophet a liar and said God had never sent him to tell them not to go down to Egypt but that Baruch had set the prophet against them. Baruch, so they said, desired that they be handed over to Nebuchadnezzar to be killed or taken prisoner to Babylon.

JEREMIAH IN EGYPT

Johanan and the other leaders carried through their rebellion against the instructions of the Lord. They took the remnant of Judah, the men, women and children with the King's daughters, Jeremiah, the prophet, and Baruch, his scribe, to Egypt and came to Tahpanhes. The word of the Lord came to Jeremiah in Tahpanhes saying:

"Take great stones in thine hand, and hide them in the clay in the brickkiln [a place for drying brick in the sun], which is at the entry of Pharaoh's house in Tahpanhes, in the sight of the men of Judah; And say unto

them, Thus saith the Lord of hosts, the God of Israel:
Behold, I will send and take Nebuchadnezzar the king
of Babylon, my servant, and will set his throne upon
these stones that I have hid: and he shall spread his
royal pavilion over them. And when he cometh, he
shall smite the land of Egypt, and deliver such as are
for death to death; and such as are for captivity to captivity; and such as are for the sword to the sword. And
I will kindle a fire in the houses of the gods of Egypt;
and he shall burn them, and carry them [the idols]
away captives: and he shall array himself with the land
of Egypt, as a shepherd putteth on his garment; and
he shall go forth from thence in peace. He shall break
also the images [obelisks] of Beth-shemesh [house or
temple of the Sun], that is in the land of Egypt; and
the houses of the gods of the Egyptians shall he burn
with fire." (Jer. 43: 9-13.)

It was for the purpose of escaping this type of destruction that the Jews had fled to Egypt. Jeremiah had
warned them that their only safety lay in remaining in
Palestine but after they had forced him to accompany
them into Egypt the Lord spoke through Jeremiah to
warn them of the certainty of the fate which awaited
them for their disobedience. Nebuchadnezzar, whom
they had hoped to escape by fleeing into Egypt, was to
come to the land of the Pharaohs and there would be
great destruction.

PALACE OF KING'S DAUGHTER

In 1886 Mr. E. Flinders Petrie unearthed at Tah-

panhes the identical palace where the royal remnant of
Judah resided in Egypt. The mound which covered
the ruins had always been associated by the Arabs with
the missing daughters of Zedekiah. Mr. Petrie found
that its remains gave evidence of having been visited
by a very sudden destruction, as by fire, and from a
thorough exploration of the premises he was equally
satisfied that the ruins had remained intact from the
time of that catastrophe until he unearthed this ancient
site. He discovered coins and pottery which enable us
to synchronize the date of its destruction with the known
era of Jeremiah. In the court yard he lay bare the very
pavement upon which Nebuchadnezzar must have
spread his royal pavilion while his army was in camp
at Daphne.

The very blocks hidden by Jeremiah in the brick kiln
were discovered by Nebuchadnezzar and used by him as
the foundation stones for his throne. These stones came
to light when found by the Arabs beneath the pavement
itself where they were undoubtedly concealed by
Nebuchadnezzar's order.

Mr. E. Flinders Petrie said:

"The first evening that I arrived there [at Tahpan-
hes], I heard to my surprise that it was known as the
Kasr el Bint el Yehudi, or the Palace of the Jew's
daughter."

Mr. Petrie continued:

"Here, if anywhere, history locates the 'Jew's daughters,' the last remnant of the Royal family recognized
as such."

EVIL PRACTICES IN EGYPT

While Jeremiah and the Royal remnant resided in Egypt at the Tahpanes, the word of the Lord came to him concerning the Jews who dwelt in Egypt. The prophet speaks of the affliction of Jerusalem, which was the misery they had witnessed, as well as the destruction of many of the cities of Judah. They were now empty and desolate for the wickedness practiced by their inhabitants. Among those wicked practices was the offering of sacrifices to gods whom they or their fathers had not known.

God had sent His prophets who had pleaded with His people to turn from their evil ways but they would not listen. As a result the land of Palestine was desolate. The question was asked of the Jews who were residing in Egypt why in the face of all these facts they continued to provoke God to anger by committing the same evils. The prophet asked them if they had forgotten the wickedness of their fathers and the kings of Judah and their wives, their own wickedness and the wickedness of their wives which had been committed in the land of Judah and in the streets of Jerusalem? Jeremiah chided them declaring they were not even then humble though all that trouble had come upon them. They were not afraid, nor did they walk in obedience to God's laws and keep His statutes which had been given to their fathers to keep and administer.

Because the Jews were continuing the evil practices in Egypt for which they had been driven out of their own land, God declared:

"I will take the remnant of Judah, that have set their faces to go into the land of Egypt to sojourn there, and they shall all be consumed, and fall in the land of Egypt: they shall even be consumed by the sword and by the famine: they shall die, from the least even unto the greatest, by the sword and by the famine; and they shall be an execration, and an astonishment, and a curse, and a reproach. For I will punish them that dwell in the land of Egypt, as I have punished Jerusalem, by the sword, by the famine, and by the pestilence." (Jer. 44: 12-13.)

Jeremiah informed these evil men that none would escape, nor would they return to the land of Judah— not even those who might leave the land of Egypt as a result of the prophet's warning.

DEFIANCE OF GOD

Then all the men who knew their wives had sacrificed to other gods, together with other women, stood up and shouted loudly that they would not listen to Jeremiah's words. They declared their intention to continue to offer sacrifices to the Queen of heaven and pour out oblations in her honor as they did in the land of Judah and in the streets of Jerusalem.

QUEEN OF HEAVEN

The worship of the Queen of Heaven so strongly condemned by Jeremiah, probably denoting moon worship, seems to be the oldest known of all religions. Not only do we find indications of it in the earliest Assyrian records, but also in Accadian accounts. Mention is made of it in the book of Job and in Genesis it is identified with that of Ashtoroth, in the name of the city of Ashtoroth-Karnaim (the two horned), where Kudur-Lagumer (Chedorlaomer) smote the gigantic Rephaim, and which was afterwards the chief city and residence of Og, King of Bashan.

The Rephaim were kin to the Nephilim (Gen. 6: 4), who were said to have been "from everlasting [me-olam], men of renown." We find evidence of moon worship in the name of Naram-Sin and in the Chaldean temple of Mullil of Nippur, the remains of which were found 22 feet beneath the site of the temple of Sargon I and Naram-Sin. Ashtoroth was identified by the Phoenicians with Juno of the Romans, and is probably the same as Ishtar and Astarte. Her worship was introduced by Jezebel among ten-tribed Israel, and its importance may be judged from the fact that no less than 400 priests were appointed for her service. Its rites are said to have been filthy in the extreme. Her temple at Aphek in Lebanon was a horrible sink of the most bestial lewdness.

ARCHEOLOGICAL EVIDENCE

Dr. Sami Gabra, a coptic acheologist, has just discovered letters in a tall stone jar written more than 2,400 years ago, the writings upon which further corroborate the text of the Bible, according to a news dispatch dated Cairo, Egypt, April 13, 1946. Each of the letters begins with a religious invocation to the pagan deities at the

Temple of Nebu at Asswan in upper Egypt and to "Malekat Shemin," the "Queen of Heaven" mentioned by Jeremiah. Here is archeological confirmation that the record of Jeremiah's condemnation of those who carried him to Egypt for worshipping these heathen gods is true.

This worship was probably the chief cause of the decadence and final extinction of several great nations, as it was most certainly that of the Seven Nations of Canaan.

Jeremiah's appeal was of no avail, for the people declared they were going to keep the oath they had made to sacrifice to the Queen of Heaven. When they did this, even in Judah, they had plenty of food and prospered, and no harm came to them. They said it was only after they had ceased these practices that they were at the mercy of the sword and famine. The women declared they had the consent of their husbands in the things they were doing.

THE PEOPLE REFUSE

The prophet answered by saying it was because of these practices committed in Judah by the king and the people that the sword had come, for God had not forgotten their evil doings:

"So the Lord could no longer bear, because of the evil of your doings, and because of the abominations which ye have committed, therefore is your land a desolation, and an astonishment, and a curse, without an inhabitant, as at this day. Because ye have burned incense, and because ye have sinned against the Lord, and have not obeyed the voice of the Lord, nor walked in his law, nor in his statutes, nor in his testimonies; therefore this evil is happened unto you, as at this day." (Jer. 44: 22-23.)

Jeremiah then addressed the people and the women who had vowed they would continue to sacrifice to the Queen of Heaven and pour out libations in her honor in spite of all he had said. He told them to keep their word and carry out their vows but listen to the word of the Lord and the judgment pronounced upon them:

"Behold, I have sworn by my great name, saith the Lord, that my name shall no more be named in the mouth of any man of Judah in the land of Egypt, saying, The Lord God liveth. Behold, I will watch over them for evil, and not for good: and all the men of Judah that are in the land of Egypt shall be consumed by the sword, and by the famine, until there be an end of them." (Jer. 44: 26-27.)

AN ESCAPING REMNANT

Following this judgment was the promise that a remnant would escape from the land of Egypt. This promise should have immediately placed every scholar on guard against committing the error of assuming Jeremiah perished in Egypt with his mission unfulfilled. That mission included the command: "to build and to plant." Up to this time the prophet had fulfilled only the first part of the mission assigned to him. In fact, the entire book of Jeremiah is devoted to the fulfillment of that part of his commission which is set forth in the statement:

"See, I have this day set thee over the nations and over the kingdoms, to root out, and to pull down, and to destroy, and to throw down." (Jer. 1: 10.)

We have been studying this phase of the prophet's work which he achieved in Palestine and in Egypt. The building and planting must of necessity be accomplished in some other place. Professor C. A. L. Totten stated:

"Jeremiah's disappearance from Eastern and sacred history, is the very reason why we should look for him in the secular history of the West where we shall find him."

The prophecy of an escaping remnant from the desolation and destruction soon to descend upon Egypt was as follows:

"Yet a small number that escape the sword shall return out of the land of Egypt into the land of Judah, and all the remnant of Judah, that are gone into the land of Egypt to sojourn there, shall know whose words shall stand, mine or their's." (Jer. 44: 28.)

When the remnant escaped from Egypt those who remained would know that God's word spoken by Jeremiah was true and the sign would be given that the punishment of which the prophet had spoken was coming upon them. Also, this would be to them evidence that Pharaoh Hophra, King of Egypt, would be given into the hands of his enemies and murderers, as Zedekiah, the King of Judah, had been given into the hands of Nebuchadnezzar, King of Babylon, his enemy.

THE PREDICTED SIGN

Jeremiah had been constrained to go down into Egypt against his will.   There he denounced those who had fallen away from Jehovah, the God of Israel, with the result that the prophet and the few who adhered to him were ostracized by the majority of the Jews who dwelt in Egypt. This perhaps contributed to his later secret flight and he and the small remnant evidently left Egypt before the Jews were aware of their disappearance. The prophet had shown the outcome of the internal conditions existing in Egypt, for the spirit of rebellion was present. The fulfillment of his prophecy that Pharaoh Hophra would die by the hand of his enemy came in the death of this Pharaoh, who was slain by his General, Ahmes.

Extensive plans had no doubt been made by Jeremiah for the escape from Egypt. Nebuchadnezzar, King of Babylon, was friendly with him and the King had made contact with Ahmes whom he confirmed as Pharaoh before he withdrew from Egypt, clothed in the spoils of this ancient land. In the general confusion resulting from the invasion of Egypt Jeremiah, with the King's daughters, Baruch, his scribe, and others, quietly slipped out of the country unobserved and unnoticed, for the God of Israel had still more work for him to do "to build and to plant." More about this later, however.

BARUCH REMINDED OF PROMISE

In the midst of his prophecies concerning Egypt the

prophet mentions Baruch's discouragement when, in the fourth year of the reign of Jehoiakim, he had finished recording the words of Jeremiah in a book. He evidently cites this reference at this time to confirm the prophecy that a remnant would escape and that Baruch would accompany Jeremiah in his flight from Egypt:

"Thus saith the Lord, the God of Israel, unto thee, O Baruch; Thou didst say [it was in the past when Jehoiakim reigned], Woe is me now! for the Lord hath added grief to my sorrow; I fainted in my sighing, and I find no rest." (Jer. 45: 2-3.)

This was evidently the time that Jehoiakim had sent messengers to take both Jeremiah and Baruch, his scribe, that they might be killed and Baruch was very much disturbed. Jeremiah was instructed to say to him:

"Behold, that which I have built will I break down, and that which.I have planted I will pluck up, even this whole land. And seekest thou great things for thyself? seek them not: for, behold, I will bring evil upon all flesh, saith the Lord: but thy life will I give unto thee for a prey in all places whither thou goest." (Jer. 45: 4-5.)

In Egypt, therefore, Baruch was again reminded that a small remnant would escape and he would be numbered among them, for God had assured him his life would be preserved. Those with Jeremiah were to live to see the fulfillment of the prophet's entire mission, including the results of the building and planting phase of his work.

CHAPTER XVI

PROPHECIES CONCERNING NATIONS AND KINGDOMS

The prophecies of Jeremiah concerning the nations and kingdoms given in his book from the forty-sixth to the fiftieth chapters, with a detailed account of the final destruction and burning of Jerusalem, are not in their chronological order. These prophecies are evidently recorded for the purpose of setting forth that phase of Jeremiah's mission when God placed him over nations and kingdoms to root out, to pull down and to destroy. For Jeremiah not only prophesied against Israel and Judah, but he also prophesied against many other nations.

PROPHECY AGAINST EGYPT

The word of the Lord came to Jeremiah to prophesy against Egypt and against the army of Pharaoh encamped near the River Euphrates in Carchemish. This was the army defeated by Nebuchadnezzar in the fourth year of the reign of Jehoiakim.

Pharaoh-necho began an invasion of Syria with a view to re-establishing Egyptian supremacy in that country. According to Ridpath's *History of the World*:

"He proceeded through the plain of Esdraelon, as far as the city of Megiddo, where he met Josiah, King of Judah, with an army drawn up to oppose his progress. Josiah was at this time tributary to Nabopolassar, and for some cause had come to prefer a Babylonian to an Egyptian master . . . The battle went against the Jewish king, who was driven, mortally wounded, into Jerusalem, where he died. Necho then proceeded with the invasion of Syria, and carried his triumphant arms to the very banks of the Euphrates.

"The authority of Egypt was thus restored over the whole western portion of the dominions which, out of the spoils of Assyria, had fallen to Nabopolassar. On his return from this successful campaign, Necho interfered in the civil war which was going on between the two sons of Josiah, both of whom claimed the crown of Judah. The Egyptian decided in favor of Jehoiakim, Jehoahaz, the younger brother, being deposed as a usurper. Before reaching his own country, Necho fell upon the strong fortress of Gaza, next to Ashdod, the principle town of Philistia, and carried it after a siege.

"Nabopolassar was now (B.C. 605) in the last year of his life. Alarmed by the loss of Syria, he determined to recover what Necho had taken from him. After the army was raised and equipped, however, the aged King found himself unable to conduct the expedition, and so the command was given to his son, Nebuchadnezzar. The prince had already had considerable experience in war, and had shown tokens of the distinguished career which awaited him. He pushed boldly into upper Syria, where at Carchemish the Egyptians had established themselves in full force to hold the country. Here they were attacked by the Babylonian army and were completely routed. Every vestige of Egyptian resistance melted away."

INVASION OF EGYPT PREDICTED

Using this defeat of the Egyptians by Babylon as an example of the helplessness of the army of Pharaoh to stand before the Babylonians, Jeremiah prophesied that Nebuchadnezzar, King of Babylon, would invade the land of Egypt, take a spoil and carry away captives. So the prophet prophesied:

"Declare ye in Egypt, and publish in Migdol, and publish in Noph [Memphis], and in Tahpanhes: say ye, Stand fast, and prepare thee; for the sword shall devour round about thee." (Jer. 46: 14.)

God, so Jeremiah said, would deliver Egypt and their gods into the hand of Nebuchadnezzar, King of Babylon. All this came to pass when Nebuchadnezzar invaded Egypt and pitched his tent at Tahpanhes where Jeremiah hid the great stones in the brick kiln.

PROPHECY CONCERNING ISRAEL

But God promised that afterward; that is, after all the judgments prononunced upon Egypt had been fulfilled, it would be inhabited again as in the days of old, and as it is today. Using this judgment upon Egypt as background, Jeremiah declared:

"But fear not thou, O my servant Jacob, and be not dismayed, O Israel: for, behold, I will save thee from afar off, and thy seed from the land of their captivity; and Jacob shall return, and be in rest and at ease, and none shall make him afraid. Fear thou not, O Jacob my servant, saith the Lord: for I am with thee; for I will make a full end of all nations whither I have driven thee; but I will not make a full end of thee, but correct thee in measure; yet will I not leave thee wholly unpunished." (Jer. 46: 27-28.)

This is a remarkable prophecy concerning the ultimate salvation of the seed of Abraham, Isaac and Jacob. It is a promise of future blessing when Israel will be at rest and none will make them afraid. The fullness of this promise has not as yet been realized, though Israel has been saved from the land of Assyria. Moving westward into Europe, and on to the Isles of the sea, Israel finally reached the appointed place where Nathan, the prophet, told David the people would have rest:

"Moreover I will appoint a place for my people Israel, and will plant them, that they may dwell in a place of their own, and move no more; neither shall the children of wickedness afflict them any more, as beforetime." (II Sam. 7: 10.)

THE DESOLATE HERITAGES

From these Isles Israel expanded and came into the inheritance of the desolate heritages of the earth as predicted by Isaiah:

"Thus saith the Lord, In an acceptable time have I heard thee, and in a day of salvation have I helped thee: and I will preserve thee, and give thee for a covenant of the people, to establish the earth, to cause to inherit the desolate heritages; That thou mayest say to the prisoners, Go forth; to them that are in darkness, Shew yourselves." (Isa. 49: 8-9.)

RETURN TO PALESTINE

The House of Jacob returned to possess their homeland again when Israel-Britain drove the Turks from Palestine. Under the protection of Israel the land is being restored. The final, complete phase of fulfillment of this prophecy is yet future. To a certain extent Great Britain and the United States are at rest and at ease and none make them afraid, but the fullness of this promise will not come until wars shall cease and the establishment of righteousness becomes a reality throughout the entire world.

The reason for these blessings is given in the statement that the Lord is with us, for though He will bring about the destruction of some nations, He will not permit the destruction of Israel. However, God has declared His people are to be corrected in a measure for, because of their sinful ways, He will not leave them wholly unpunished. This period of punishment is the time of Jacob's trouble, reference to which has already been made (see Chapter 11, *The New Covenant*).

While God is pronouncing judgment upon Israel through His prophets, He also permits them to look forward to the day of Israel's redemption when, cleansed of all evil, they will be worthy to receive the promised blessings.

TIME OF PROPHECIES

The judgments pronounced upon the nations were

evidently the messages Jeremiah sent to the various kings whose ambassadors had gathered at Jerusalem at the beginning of Zedekiah's reign to discuss ways and means of breaking the yoke of Babylon (see Chapter 10, *Jeremiah's Controversy With the Preachers*). These judgments are recorded here as a permanent record of the calamities that would overtake those countries. History has since corroborated every prediction.

THE PHILISTINES

The forty-seventh chapter of Jeremiah is the judgment God pronounced against the Philistines before Pharaoh overcame Gaza. This judgment was fulfilled in every respect as history completely verifies.

JUDGMENT UPON MOAB

The next chapter deals with the judgment pronounced upon Moab because they trusted in their works and treasure. They are described as being at ease and never having gone into captivity. But God declares that because Moab had magnified himself against the Lord his people would also become a derision. Restoration, however, is promised in the latter days.

THE AMMONITES

Next the prophet deals with the Ammonites. The question is asked:

"Hath Israel no sons? hath he no heir? why then doth their king inherit Gad, and his people dwell in his cities?" (Jer. 49: 1.)

This is an interesting prophecy of a time to come when

the House of Israel, who, at the time Jeremiah was speaking, had been carried away to Assyria, would have sons to inherit the cities of Ammon. Not only would they inherit the cities of Ammon but Israel would dominate those who formerly dominated them. Today Great Britain has come into possession of the ancient land of Ammon.

Meantime, Ammon was to be driven out of their land but the promise is made that a day would come when the Lord would restore the fortunes of the Ammonites.

CONCERNING EDOM

The question is asked:

"Is wisdom no more in Teman? is counsel perished from the prudent? is their wisdom vanished?" (Jer. 49: 7.)

Edom is Esau (Gen. 36: 9) and Teman, a city in Edom, was also the name of a grandson of Esau (Gen. 36: 11). Wisdom and counsel had evidently disappeared from Esau's descendants and God declares He will bring doom upon Esau as the hour of punishment approached. The overthrow of Edom is likened to the overthrow of Sodom and Gomorrah. Ezekiel also prophesied concerning Edom and said:

"And I will lay my vengeance upon Edom by the hand of my people Israel: and they shall do in Edom according to mine anger and according to my fury; and they shall know my vengeance, saith the Lord. (Ez. 25: 14.)

While Nebuchadnezzar was used of God to bring about the fulfillment of judgment upon Edom in his day, the prophecy itself as given by Ezekiel looks to the distant future for its complete fulfillment. Students of prophecy have believed this prediction of Ezekiel's became history when Israel-Britain advanced from Egypt against the Turks (Edom), driving them from Palestine and taking the city of Jerusalem in 1917 A.D. This conclusion is born out by Jeremiah's prophecy in which he indicated the line of march as the British forces come up from the south:

"Behold, he shall come up like a lion from the swelling of Jordan against the habitation of the strong: but I will suddenly make him run away from her." (Jer. 49: 19.)

The Turks did suddenly run away from the British forces and Jerusalem fell to General Allenby without the city being demolished by an attack. Jeremiah predicted:

"Behold, he shall come up and fly as the eagle, and spread his wings over Bozrah: and at that day shall the heart of the mighty men of Edom be as the heart of a woman in her pangs." (Jer. 49: 22.)

As the eagle flies, so the airplanes appeared over Bozrah, causing the Turks to flee. Thus, the prophecy was fulfilled that the mighty men of Edom would be in great fear.

CONCERNING DAMASCUS

Damascus is spoken of as being confounded with her

young men falling in the streets and a fire consuming the city walls and palaces. Nebuchadnezzar is shown as the one whom God would use to bring judgment upon these nations in the day of calamity. History amply testifies to the accuracy of Jeremiah's predictions as the King of Babylon conquered and destroyed the cities of the nations which resisted him.

ELAM

The record states that this prophecy concerning Elam was made in the beginning of the reign of Zedekiah, King of Judah. According to *Young's Analytical Concordance*, Elam is Persia and Jeremiah declared that in the latter days Elam would be restored. If the identity is correct, this prophecy has been fulfilled, for Persia is in existence today though many of the nations of whom Jeremiah was speaking do not now exist.

Evidently this prophecy regarding Elam was delivered by Jeremiah to the Ambassador from Persia present with the representatives of other nations at the time a counsel was being held in Jerusalem when they were trying to find ways and means to throw off the yoke of Babylon. Others present at the time, to whose kings messages were sent, were Edom, Moab, Ammon, Tyrus and Zidon. Ambassadors of other nations might also have been present whose names are not given in the record, as Elam's name was not given in the original account of the conference recorded in the twenty-seventh chapter of Jeremiah.

JUDGMENT UPON BABYLON

God declares that Israel is His battle-axe and weapons of war but Babylon is called the "hammer of the whole earth" (Jer. 50: 23). This hammer is to be broken and judgment is pronounced upon Babylon. The prophet not only shows the overthrow of ancient Babylon, but he also includes in these prophecies of judgment the overthrow of the entire Babylonian system as it extends from the time of ancient Babylon to the end of the Times of the Gentiles. This is borne out by the statement that in the complete destruction of Babylon Israel will be restored to full covenant relationship with Jehovah, the God of Israel. This did not take place when ancient Babylon fell, but it is to take place when the entire Babylonian system passes away. Accordingly, the prophet proclaims the message:

"Declare ye among the nations, and publish, and set up a standard; publish, and conceal not: say, Babylon is taken, Bel is confounded, Merodach is broken in pieces; her idols are confounded, her images are broken in pieces. For out of the north there cometh up a nation against her, which shall make her land desolate, and none shall dwell therein: they shall remove, they shall depart, both man and beast." (Jer. 50: 2-3.)

While we recognize the fact that the prophecy was fulfilled in the destruction of ancient Babylon by the Medes and Persians, the full prediction here given remains to be fulfilled in its entirety with the ending of the Times of the Gentiles.

FOUR PHASES OF ACTIVITY

Four phases of Babylonian activity, upon which judgment is to come, are set forth in this prophecy. The destruction of the ancient Babylonian Empire did not destroy Babylonian influence, represented in its political, military, religious and economic phases of activity. According to Jeremiah all these manifestations are to finally pass away.

In the statement, "Babylon is taken," we have a prophecy of the destruction of Babylon's political power. When the prophet refers to the fact that Bel is confounded, it is a reference to confusion in the religious phase of Babylonian activity, for Bel is a contraction of the Aramaic form of *Baal*, the national god of Babylon. The statement that Merodach is broken in pieces is a prophecy of the complete destruction of the military might and power of Babylon, for Merodach was the Babylonian god of war. The reference to the idols being confounded and the images broken is a prophecy of the judgment upon the Babylonian economy. It was the image of gold, the winged disk, which Nebuchadnezzar set up as the standard of commercial activity.* Nations have been worshipping the gold standard ever since the day Nebuchadnezzar set this image up on the plains of Dura and money, which it represents, has become the coveted idol of all.

END OF GENTILE RULE

The scope of Jeremiah's prophecy concerning Baby-

---

* See *Study in Revelation,* page 274.   Price $5.00 postpaid.
DESTINY Publishers, Merrimac, Mass. 01860

lon extends to the very end of the age when, as declared by John in Revelation, full judgment will come upon the Babylonian system and its activities in all of their manifestations. For a more complete discussion of the modern manifestation of Babylon, the reader is referred to the book, *Study in Revelation.*

The following is quoted from "End of Gentile Rule," DESTINY for July, 1945:

"Daniel interpreted a most interesting vision in which Nebuchadnezzar was shown an image of a man symbolizing coming world empires. Daniel informed the King that those empires would begin with Babylon and would be followed by nations which history has revealed to be Medo-Persia, Greece, Imperial Rome and finally, as represented by the feet, the subdivisions of the Roman Empire in Continental Europe.

"In vision the King saw a stone cut out of the mountain without hands which smote the image upon its feet breaking, destroying and grinding to powder this image of world empires. Now this Stone Kingdom began to strike the feet of the image when our forces invaded Italy (see "Hitting the Feet of Clay," DESTINY for August, 1945) and with the collapse of Germany the smashing and grinding process was completed, for in the unconditional surrender of the Nazis the Babylonian Succession of Empires ended. Politically and militarily Babylon had fallen!

"The Times of the Gentiles were fulfilled with the beginning of World War I, and now the judgment of military Babylon has been completed with the destruction of the military power and might of Germany. During this final phase of Gentile activity the Nazis succeeded in taking over most of Europe, spreading out into Africa and to the shores of the Black Sea. This end of the Babylonian Succession of Empires is a terminal of major importance to students of prophecy, for now the way is open for the final Armageddon contest.

"Standing across the path of Israel's greatness, Soviet Russia intends to challenge the right of Israel to her inheritance and will by war seek to destroy her to prevent the Kingdom from possessing its God-given heritage . . .

"The curtain has fallen on the activities of the Babylonian Succession and is now being raised on the greatest of all dramas, revealing the organization of a confederacy which is moving to challenge God as to world rulership. God has accepted that challenge and the scenes upon the stage of world affairs will be thrilling indeed to watch for those who know the pattern of things to come."

Though the military power of Babylon is broken, and the political activities have passed away, there yet remains judgment upon its religious and economic phases of activity. Already we are witnessing confusion and uncertainty in the religious and economic world, while judgment is coming upon our present economic structure. John, in Revalation, refers to the different stages in this process of judgment, the detail of which will be found in *Study in Revelation*.

GATHERING OF ISRAEL

It is certain that Jeremiah had in view this broader aspect of the fall of Babylon, in addition to the immediate fulfillment of his prophecy, for he declared:

"In those days, and in that time, saith the Lord, the children of Israel shall come, they and the children of Judah together, going and weeping: they shall go, and seek the Lord their God. They shall ask the way to Zion with their faces thitherward, saying, Come, and let us join ourselves to the Lord in a perpetual covenant that shall not be forgotten." (Jer. 50: 4-5.)

All the prophets point out that when Israel returns to God in that way it will be the end of the age and the beginning of a new order. This is the day, according to Ezekiel, of which the Lord declares:

"Then will I sprinkle clean water upon you, and ye shall be clean: from all your filthiness, and from all your idols, will I cleanse you. A new heart also will I give you, and a new spirit will I put within you: and I will take away the stony heart out of your flesh, and I will give you an heart of flesh. And I will put my spirit within you, and cause you to walk in my statutes, and ye shall keep my judgments, and do them." (Ez. 36: 25-27.)

This prophecy was not fulfilled when ancient Babylon fell, and only now are we approaching the day of its fulfillment. Because Israel has been blind and has wandered away, God charges the shepherds and leaders in Israel with the responsibility for having led His sheep astray:

"My people hath been lost sheep: their shepherds have caused them to go astray, they have turned them away on the mountains: they have gone from mountain to hill, they have forgotten their restingplace. All that found them have devoured them: and their adversaries said, We offend not, because they have sinned against the Lord, the habitation of justice; even the Lord, the hope of their fathers." (Jer. 50: 6-7.)

Through the prophet Ezekiel God declares Israel shall never again be a prey and will dwell safely, none making them afraid (Ez. 34: 28). This confirms Jeremiah's statement that this is to be the state of Israel in the time of restoration. Ezekiel further declares:

"Thus shall they know that I the Lord their God am with them, and that they, even the house of Israel, are my people, saith the Lord God. And ye my flock, the flock of my pasture, are men, and I am your God, saith the Lord God." (Ez. 34: 30-31.)

A CALL TO LEAVE BABYLON

The prophet next issued a call for Israel to come out of the midst of Babylon and leave the land of the Chaldeans. This also has a double application, for it was not only addressed to those residing in ancient Babylon, but to Israel of the latter days as well. John repeats this call, but he is admonishing God's people to leave the evils of the Babylonian system:

"Come out of her, my people, that ye be not partakers of her sins, and that ye receive not of her plagues." (Rev. 18: 4.)

Destruction is pronounced as coming upon Babylon from the north as a great nation assembles to overthrow her and take a spoil. This, too, has a double application, for while ancient Babylon was overthrown by the Medes and Persians, modern Babylon fell in the defeat of Germany by the Allied Nations, one of whom was Soviet Russia, a northern nation of modern times.

It is difficult to separate the judgments pronounced upon Babylon into the part applicable to ancient Babylon alone and that which applies to the Succession of Babylonian Empires, which comes at the end of the Times of the Gentiles.

BABYLON REJOICES

Jeremiah refers to the rejoicing in Babylon over the destruction of God's heritage (His kingdom people), for both ancient Babylon and its modern counterpart, Nazi-Germany, rejoiced in the destruction wrought upon Israel. God declares:

"Israel is a scattered sheep; the lions have driven him away: first the king of Assyria hath devoured him [the House of Israel disappeared in the land of Assyria]; and last this Nebuchadnezzar king of Babylon hath broken his bones. Therefore thus saith the Lord of hosts, the God of Israel; Behold, I will punish the king of Babylon and his land, as I have punished the king of Assyria. And I will bring Israel again to his habitation, and he shall feed on Carmel and Bashan, and his soul shall be satisfied upon mount Ephraim and Gilead. In those days, and in that time, saith the Lord, the iniquity of Israel shall be sought for, and there shall be none; and the sins of Judah, and they shall not be found: for I will pardon them whom I reserve." (Jer. 50: 17-20.)

In pronouncing judgment upon Babylon, Jeremiah declares that because they have striven against God:

"The Lord hath opened his armoury, and hath brought forth the weapons of his indignation." (Jer. 50: 25.)

GOD'S HAMMER

The prophet describes a sound of battle in the land with great destruction. Though Babylon had been the hammer, or breaker of nations, she was to be broken herself. He calls for the utter destruction of this great city, for the time of its visitation had come. Because the children of Israel had been oppressed and their captors had refused to let them go, Jeremiah pointed out:

"Their Redeemer is strong; the Lord of hosts is his name: he shall thoroughly plead their cause, that he may give rest to the land, and disquiet the inhabitants of Babylon." (Jer. 50: 34.)

ISRAEL'S CAPTORS

Who are Israel's captors? We know that both ancient Assyria and Babylon can be so classified, but what of the modern oppressors of His people? Is not Israel today subject to an oppressive economy, making life for multitudes worse in some respects than the Egyptian slavery of His people?

The evils of the present economy, with its system of excess taxation confiscating the possessions and earnings of the people, has become such an integral part of our modern way of life that only through the intervention of the Lord of Hosts Himself can the bonds of this servitude be broken. Jeremiah prophesied that the Re deemer of Israel will fully plead the cause of His people and give rest to their land, bringing discomfiture upon those who are responsible for oppressing them. Ezekiel refers to the time when, following the defeat of Gog, of the land of Magog (the Communist hordes), God's people Israel shall:

"Spoil those that spoiled them, and rob those that robbed them, saith the Lord God." (Ez. 39: 10.)

Following this Ezekiel prophesies of the restoration of Israel when God will pour out His spirit upon the House of Israel.

Jeremiah calls for a sword upon Babylon, upon its inhabitants, princes and wise men. The waters of Babylon are to dry up, the wild beasts of the desert shall dwell there and it shall not be inhabited again nor be dwelt in from generation to generation:

"Therefore hear ye the counsel of the Lord, that he hath taken against Babylon; and his purposes, that he hath purposed against the land of the Chaldeans: Surely the least of the flock shall draw them out: surely he shall make their habitation desolate with them. At the noise of the taking of Babylon the earth is moved, and the cry is heard among the nations." (Jer. 50: 45-46.)

SCOPE OF JUDGMENT

The very scope of the judgment pronounced against Babylon clearly indicates that Jeremiah's prophecy was not confined to the destruction of the ancient city, but included the entire period of Babylonian activity to the very end of the age when the Times of the Gentiles should cease. This is borne out further in the prophet's statement:

"Babylon hath been a golden cup in the Lord's hand, that made all the earth drunken: the nations have drunken of her wine; therefore the nations are mad." (Jer. 51: 7.)

The fall of ancient Babylon was heard throughout the then known world as the first great world empire in the Babylonian Succession of Empires passed away. But the fall of Babylon the Great, as described by John in Revelation, has an even more profound effect upon all nations, for in its destruction the very foundation upon which our present world economy rests will pass away. John states:

"And the merchants of the earth shall weep and mourn over her; for no man buyeth their merchandise any more . . . And they cast dust on their heads, and cried, weeping and wailing, saying, Alas, alas that great city, wherein were made rich all that had ships in the sea by reason of her costliness! for in one hour is she made desolate." (Rev. 18: 11 & 19.)

The prophet affirms the certainty of this judgment by declaring that the Lord of Hosts hath sworn by Himself that He will perform His word upon Babylon.

ISRAEL'S PORTION

The prophet refers to God's power, wisdom and knowledge. He labels the makers of idols as ignorant men who are confounded by the idols which they fashion, for they are lies without souls. He calls them vain and the work of delusions, for in the season of trial they have no power to help. The prophet declares that the portion of Jacob is not like them:

"He is the former of all things: and Israel is the rod of his inheritance: the Lord of hosts is his name." (Jer. 51: 19.)

Continuing to address Israel, the Lord, through His prophet, states:

"Thou art my battle axe and weapons of war: for with thee will I break in pieces the nations, and with thee will I destroy kingdoms." (Jer. 51: 20.)

There are those who have tried to apply this verse to Babylon but Babylon is God's hammer, not His battle-axe, while the one addressed in this verse is the observer of the judgment which will come upon Babylon:

"And I will render unto Babylon and to all the inhabitants of Chaldea all their evil that they have done in Zion in your sight, saith the Lord." (Jer. 51: 24.)

The fact that Israel is to be God's battle-axe and weapons of war to break nations in pieces and destroy kingdoms is apparent from Daniel's statement:

"And in the days of these kings shall the God of heaven set up a kingdom, which shall never be destroyed: and the kingdom shall not be left to other people, but it shall break in pieces and consume all these kingdoms, and it shall stand for ever." (Dan. 2: 44.)

THE HAMMER BROKEN

God's hammer, Babylon, is to be broken but His battle-axe, Israel, is to stand forever. Continuing now with the description in detail of the judgment upon Babylon, as God moves to avenge His people, the prophet states:

"Therefore thus saith the Lord; Behold, I will plead thy cause, and take vengeance for thee [Jerusalem]; and I will dry up her sea [river], and make her springs dry. And Babylon shall become heaps, a dwellingplace for dragons, an astonishment and an hissing, without an inhabitant." (Jer. 51: 36-37.)

Of the princes, wise men, captains and rulers of Babylon, Jeremiah declares:

"They shall sleep a perpetual sleep, and not wake, saith the King, whose name is the Lord of hosts. Thus saith the Lord of hosts; The broad walls of Babylon shall be utterly broken, and her high gates shall be burned with fire." (Jer. 51: 57-58.)

FULFILLED PROPHECY

The following account was published in DESTINY for October, 1942 and clearly illustrates how complete was the judgment both Isaiah and Jeremiah prophesied would come upon the ancient city of Babylon:

"A Colonel in the Turkish army once asked Dr. Cyrus Hamlin for a proof that the Bible is the word of

God. Learning that the Colonel had been a great traveler, Dr. Hamlin said to him, 'Have you ever been in Babylon?'

" 'Yes,' said the Colonel, 'and I will tell you a curious incident. The ruins of Babylon abound in game, and, wishing for a week's shooting, I engaged a Sheik with his followers and went there. At sundown the Arabs, to my amazement, began to strike their tents. I went to the Sheik and protested most strongly; I was paying him handsomely, and I now offered to double the amount; but nothing I could say had any effect.

" 'It is not safe,' said the Sheik, 'no mortal flesh dare stay here after sunset. Ghosts and ghouls come out of the holes and caverns after dark, and whomsoever they catch becomes one of themselves. *No Arab had ever seen the sun go down on Babylon!'* "

"Dr. Hamlin then took out his Bible and read from Isaiah 13: 19, 'And Babylon, the glory of kingdoms, the beauty of the Chaldean's pride, shall be as when God overthrew Sodom and Gomorrah. It shall never be inhabited, neither shall it be dwelt in from generation to generation; *neither shall the Arabian pitch his tent there* . . . but the wild beasts of the desert shall lie there . . . and wolves shall cry in their castles, and jackals in the pleasant places.'

" 'That is the history you have been reading,' said the Turk.

" 'No,' said Dr. Hamlin, 'it is a prophecy. Those words were written when Babylon was in all her glory; you know what Babylon is today.'

"The Colonel had not a word to say in reply. Babylon was a wonderful city. Her area was five times as large as London. Her wall was at least eighty feet thick and three hundred feet high, with five hundred gates of burnished brass. Enclosed were lakes, parks and 625 city squares. The prophet Jeremiah had said of her: 'Though Babylon *shall mount up to heaven,* and though she shall *fortify the height* of her strength, yet from me shall spoilers come unto her, saith the Lord.' (Jer. 51: 53.)

"Now the above is a remarkable proof of the truth of the Bible; there are hundreds more, and these are being added to in a very remarkable manner by discoveries on inscriptions and writings which have long been buried."

VIOLENT DESTRUCTION

Jeremiah wrote in a book all the evil that was to come upon Babylon and gave the book to Seraiah who went with Zedekiah to Babylon. The prophet instructed him, when he came to the city, to read all the words in the city and:

"Then shalt thou say, O Lord, thou hast spoken against this place, to cut it off, that none shall remain in it, neither man nor beast, but that it shall be desolate for ever." (Jer. 51: 62.)

After reading the book and pronouncing judgment in the city he was to take a stone, bind it to the book and cast the book into the Euphrates river:

"And thou shalt say, Thus shall Babylon sink, and

shall not rise from the evil that I will bring upon her."
(Jer. 51: 64.)

In describing the violence of the overthrow of the
entire Babylonian system, particularly in reference to
the destruction of the economic phase of that system,
John sees a mighty angel take up a stone like a great
millstone, and cast it into the sea, saying:

"Thus with violence shall that great city Babylon
be thrown down, and shall be found no more at all."
(Rev. 18: 21.)

The fifty-first chapter of Jeremiah closes with the
statement, "Thus far are the words of Jeremiah," indicating the end of the prophet's message insofar as the
book of Jeremiah was concerned. It seems very fitting
that the last words of Jeremiah should deal with the
destruction of Babylon, for the age will end, according
to John, with the final overthrow of the entire Babylonian structure.

The last chapter of Jeremiah's book is a short outline of the account of the fall of Jerusalem. This record
was either written by Ezra, or someone else, and ap-
pended to the writings of Jeremiah. It shows what happened to Jerusalem, the Temple and the people of
Judea, as well as describing the elevation of Jehoiachin
in Babylon, whose line was preserved for a specific purpose. The account, as recorded by this writer, is as follows:

"Zedekiah was one and twenty years old when he
begin to reign, and he reigned eleven years in Jeru-

salem. And his mother's name was Hamutal the daughter of Jeremiah of Libnah." (Jer. 52: 1.)

For a discussion on Jeremiah's relationship to Zedekiah, King of Judah, see Chapter eight, *The Message to the House of David*. Because Jeremiah's daughter was the mother of Zedekiah, it accounts for the fact that the daughters of Zedekiah became his wards and he was charged with the responsibility of caring for them.

The writer of this last chapter in the book of Jeremiah declares that, because of Zedekiah's evil ways in the sight of God and, as a result of his rebellion against the King of Babylon:

"It came to pass in the ninth year of his reign, in the tenth month, in the tenth day of the month, that Nebuchadnezzar king of Babylon came, he and all his army, against Jerusalem." (Jer. 52: 4.)

The city was besieged into the eleventh year of Zedekiah when, as a result of the famine in the city, it fell to Nebuchadnezzar. It has already been pointed out that Zedekiah fled but was overtaken and brought before Nebuchadnezzar. His sons were slain and his eyes put out, after which he was carried to Babylon in chains and imprisoned there till the day of his death.

TEMPLE DESTROYED

Following the capture of Jerusalem the city was burned, the walls of the city were broken down and its inhabitants carried away captive. Only a few of the very poorest were left in the land.

The Temple was destroyed, the pillars of brass and the brazen sea were broken up, and all the brass taken to Babylon. Also, other furnishings, as well as the gold of the Temple, were taken to Babylon.

THE ELEVATION OF JEHOIACHIN

This chapter closes with the account of the elevation of Jehoiachin (Coniah) in Babylon. He was taken from prison and his garments changed, for the King of Babylon (Evil-merodach) spoke kindly to him and placed him above all the kings who were with him in Babylon. God has a purpose in the good fortune of Jehoiachin, see Chapter nine, *The Baskets of Good and Bad Figs*, for his posterity furnished the line from which our Lord came (see Appendix, *Which Genealogy?*).

While this ends the book of Jeremiah, it is not the record of the end of Jeremiah's mission. The building and planting which he was to accomplish was carried on beyond the confines of Palestine and Egypt. The record of this part of his activities will not be found in the sacred writings so we must look for it elsewhere. It will be found in secular history, for Jeremiah's life work really lay still ahead of him when he went down into Egypt, in the fulfillment of the final phase of his commission: *to build and to plant*.

AN ESCAPING REMNANT

It is this part of Jeremiah's life work with which we will deal in the next and final chapter of *Study in Jeremiah*. Because ecclesiastical leaders and students of the

Bible have lacked sufficient faith, they assume, without any evidence to substantiate that assumption except that Jeremiah disappeared from the sacred records after the account of his sojourn in Egypt, that this prophet perished there.

They forget that Jeremiah prophesied that a remnant would escape from Egypt and there is every good reason to believe that Jeremiah, with a little band in-including Baruch, Ebed-melech, the Ethiopian whose life God promised to spare, and the King's daughters, left for an undisclosed destination which was a closely guarded secret as the prophet prepared for this departure. God has already declared through the prophet that they would not return to reside in Palestine but would seek a divinely selected destination which was the place where Jeremiah would accomplish his building and planting.

CHAPTER XVII

BUILDING AND PLANTING

We now come to the most important part of Jeremiah's mission. It concerns the task God assigned to him to build and to plant. The first part of his mission was carried out in Palestine and finally in Egypt. He was hated by his countrymen because he told them the truth, denouncing their sins and calling upon them to restore righteousness in the nation.

The holy Scriptures are silent concerning Jeremiah's whereabouts after describing his journey to and sojourn in Egypt. But we do know that the Bible records only the fulfillment of the first part of the prophet's mission:

"See, I have this day set thee over the nations and over the kingdoms, to root out, and to pull down, and to destroy, and to throw down, to build and to plant." (Jer. 1: 10.)

Jeremiah accomplished in its entirety the destructive phase of his commission and we have every reason to believe God would see to it that he was preserved to accomplish the building and planting for which he was also commissioned. The daughters of Zedekiah became the prophet's wards and because God had promised that his covenant would not be broken with David, that he would never lack a man to reign upon his Throne, the building and planting obviously had to do with preserving this royal branch of the House of David.

DAUGHTERS OF ZELOPHEHAD

When Nebuchadnezzar killed the sons of Zedekiah, allowing his daughters to go free, he did not know of the Israel law. Under a decision rendered by the Lord in the matter of the daughters of Zelophehad, a judgment was incorporated into the Israel Law of Inheritance to provide for the daughters so that they might inherit as though they were males when there were no sons. The case of Zelophehad's daughters was presented to Moses when they appeared before him and demanded an inheritance in the land, for their father died leaving no sons:

"And the Lord spake unto Moses, saying, The daughters of Zelophehad speak right: thou shalt surely give them a possession of an inheritance among their father's brethren; and thou shalt cause the inheritance of their father to pass unto them." (Num. 27: 6-7.)

The judgment was laid down:

"And thou shalt speak unto the children of Israel, saying, If a man die, and have no son, then ye shall cause his inheritance to pass unto his daughter. And if he have no daughter, then ye shall give his inheritance unto his brethren. And if he have no brethren, then ye shall give his inheritance unto his father's brethren. And if his father have no brethren, then ye shall give his inheritance unto his kinsman that is next to him of his family, and he shall possess it: and it shall be unto the children of Israel a statute of judgment, as the Lord commanded Moses." (Num. 27: 8-11.)

DAUGHTER OF ZEDEKIAH

Zedekiah's sons were killed so there were no male heirs to the throne. Under the above law a daughter would inherit as though she were a son and the right of descent would pass to her. This fact was evidently unknown to Nebuchadnezzar who thought that in slaying Zedekiah's sons he had destroyed every heir to the Throne of David. It became Jeremiah's responsibility to see to it that the Throne of David was established in the appointed place.

ESCAPING REMNANT

While Jeremiah prophesied that those who had gone down into Egypt would be destroyed by the sword and famine, he also said, "For none shall return *but such as shall escape*" (Jer. 44: 14), indicating that a remnant would leave. The prophet also declared that the Lord would not prevent evil from befalling those who had gone down into the land of the Pharaohs against His command but he qualified this statement by referring again to a small number who would escape (Jer. 44: 28).

At an earlier date, during the time the prophet was experiencing troubles and turmoil in the violent opposition he was meeting from his countrymen, he exclaimed:

"Woe is me, my mother, that thou hast borne a man of strife and a man of contention to the whole earth! I have never lent on usury, nor men have lent to me on usury; yet every one of them doth curse me." (Jer. 15: 10.)

The Lord then said to Jeremiah:

"Verily it shall be well with thy remnant; verily I will cause the enemy to entreat thee well in the time of evil and in the time of affliction." (Jer. 15: 11.)

UNKNOWN LAND

This statement is followed by the promise that Jeremiah would pass into a land which he did not know. Where was this unknown land to which he was to go? Before answering this question, let us review the statements of other prophets. Isaiah tells us of a remnant that was to go forth from Jerusalem and escape from Zion, of whom he says:

"And the remnant that is escaped of the house of Judah shall again take root downward, and bear fruit upward." (Isa. 37: 31.)

These promises are entirely overlooked by those who seek to end Jeremiah's career in Egypt. It is well known that Jeremiah was fully alive to the importance of securing every evidence which might be of value in carrying on his work. He could not begin the building and planting until after the fall of Jerusalem and the dethronement of Zedekiah. This part of his mission must be completed somewhere, evidently somewhere other than in Palestine or Egypt. He could no more fail to accomplish this, or avoid its deliberate undertaking, if he was Jehovah's agent, than he could prevent the preceding and predicted destruction of Jerusalem and Egypt to which he bore testimony.

Long before the days of Ezekiel and Jeremiah,

Nathan told David of this place of planting (II Sam.
7: 10). We have already referred to Jeremiah's purchase of the title deeds to Anathoth, concealing them
prior to his departure from the land. To date this hid·
den evidence of Jehovah's right to Palestine has never
been produced, for they were to continue in concealment
for many days (Jer. 32: 14-15), a period which evi·-
dently has not yet run out.

TEA TEPHI

Jeremiah had every means at his command to fulfill
his mission, for he was as greatly honored and respected
by the King of Babylon as he was persecuted by his
countrymen, who looked upon him as a traitor. After
the capture of the city by the armies of Babylon, Jeremiah could go where he liked and do as he liked, and
Bible history traces him to Egypt with the King's
daughters where he vanished from Biblical records.

The signs of Jeremiah in Egypt are his own writings
and the testimony of the Jews, all of which was corroborated by E. Flinders Petrie. Jeremiah disappeared
with an escaped remnant from Jewish sight out of
Egypt. That he doubtless visited Palestine to complete
his work in gathering certain relics to be taken by him
to the far country is clear from the record of the things
he had with him when he arrived in that far country.
Following the disappearance of Jeremiah from Egypt,
there appears in western history a man with a group of
people who answer in every respect to the description
of Jeremiah and the remnant—who had with them

certain valuable possessions. The evidence of all this from Irish history would fill a volume.

To enumerate a few of the recorded facts, we have Tea Tephi (whose name means "tender twig"), a Princess from the East, coming to Ireland at this time. She was known as the King's daughter and her guardian was the prophet, Ollam Folla. With them was the Urim and Thummin breast plate, or the Jordan Moran, and the Stone of Destiny, or Lia Fail, which accompanied them to this Isle in the sea. The Harp of David hung in Tara's Halls and the evidence also bears out the claim that the Ark of the Covenant accompanied this remnant to the Isles.

The *Irish Chronicles* record the fact of the coming of an Eastern Princess. In these chronicles appears an interesting poem purporting to set forth the facts told by this Princess:

"We were five that rode upon asses,
    And five by the mules they led
Whereon were the things brought forth
    From the House of God when we fled;
The Stone of Jacob our father
    The seat wherein Yahveh dwells
Upon Sacred things whereof the Book of the Prophets
        tells
    And the signs of my father David,
On whom was the promise stayed
    Bright as the crown of the dawn,
Deep as the midnight shade,

Upon me was that promise fallen.
  For me was the Prophet's toil.
He had signed me with David's signet,
  Anointed my head with oil.
He had set my hands to the Harp;
  He had bidden me hold the spear [scepter];
The buckler was girt to my bosom,
  And Barach and he drew near
To set my feet upon Bethel,
  The stone that is seen this day.
That my seed may rest upon it
  Where'er it is borne away:
And its promises be sure beneath them,
  Strong to uphold their throne;
Though the builders cast it aside,
  It shall never be left alone."

PHAREZ AND ZARAH

Let us pause here to briefly outline the history of the
Zarah branch of Judah's posterity. Judah had two sons
by Tamar, named Pharez and Zarah. When Jacob and
his family went down into Egypt Zarah as yet had no
children. Pharez was accompanied by two sons, Hezron
and Hamul. Two sons, Ethan and Zimri, were born to
Zarah in Egypt. Ethan profited by the opportunities he
received in the land and so did his son Mahol, who also
enjoyed the same advantages. Their success won them
much fame so that they are named in connection with
Solomon whose wisdom did exceed theirs:

"And Solomon's wisdom excelled the wisdom of all

the children of the east country, and all the wisdom of Egypt. For he was wiser than all men; than Ethan the Ezrahite, and Heman, and Chalcol, and Darda, the sons of Mahol: and his fame was in all nations round about." (I Kings 4: 30-31.)

ZARAH'S AMBITIONS

It seems certain that the family of Zarah aspired to the sceptral honors of Judah but failed to attain their ambitions, and Zarah's entire household seems to have moved out of Goshen. The three sons of Mahol evidently were schooled in all the wisdom of Egypt as was Moses.

Professor C. A. L. Totten states:

"Where the Sacred Canon (purposely, as we believe) allows the record of Zarah's line to lapse, there they are blindly taken up and continued by no less than three, perhaps more, independent and widely separated secular colleges of history.

"For if Darda, the Egyptian, son of Zarah, was Dardanus, the Egyptian founder of Troy, and if Cholcol was the Egyptian Cerops or Niul and the contemporary founder of Athens and Thebes, and if Heman, the brother of Niul, was likewise contemporary Egyptian Agenon who inherited Phoenicia, and if Mahol, the son of Zarah and the father of these famous Egyptians, was Scytha, or Fenesia Farsa, the Egyptian ancestor of the Milesians, whose records, full and complete, enable us to blend the whole into one continuous recital down to the present day, surely we have means at hand in Trojan, Grecian and Milesian sources, to continue out the record of the Sacred Chronicles, and lend them greater reverence as we come to understand and prize them at their worth!

"And it is just this claim that we now advance, for by rescuing this fragmentary reference to Zarah's line, found in I Kings (4: 30-31), from the ignorance and misconception with which all former generations seem to have treated it, and by reading in it a clear and intentional reference to the famous Heroes of Secular History, to the founders of Phoenicia, Grecia, Troy, and the Milesians, and indirectly to Rome, the child of Troy, to Carthage and to the Brigantes of Hispania, we place in the hands of our race, and before their opened eyes the peer of the Rosetta Stone itself." (*The Secret of History*, page 164-166.)

JEREMIAH IN IRELAND

There are two distinct phases to the Hebrew story concerning Ireland. One deals with the Milesian records, the history of which line originated in Egypt and Palestine, while the other line concerns Jeremiah and the King's daughters, one of whom married Eochaidh, the Heremonn of the line of Zarah, upon her arrival with the Prophet in Ireland.

All the authorities agree in stating the following facts that at this time (*circa* 583 B.C.) a "notable man," an "important personage," a patriarch, a saint, an essentially important one, according to the various ways of putting it, came to Ulster, the most northern province of Ireland, accompanied by a princess, the daughter of an eastern king; and that in company with them was one Simon Brach, Breck, Barech, Berach, as it is differently spelled; and that this royal party brought with them many remarkable things. Among these were the harp, the ark and a wonderful stone called Lia Fail, or stone of destiny.

THE CORONATION CEREMONY

Just at this time as Jeremiah, with the King's daughter, his ward, arrived in Ireland, a ceremony was taking place. Under the laws of Ireland, and according to the ritual of Druidism, Eochaidh, the Heremonn, a Prince of the Tuatha de Danaans on his mother's side and a direct descendant also of Fenesia Farsa, and thus of the line of Zarah, twin brother of Pharez of the Royal House of Judah, was about to receive national recognition as the "crown Horseman" of the four principalities of Ireland.

God had removed the crown from the head of Zedekiah of the line of Pharez and placed it upon the head of a Prince of the line of Zarah who at this time was united in marriage with the daughter of Zedekiah, heir to David's Throne. Here, then, the prophet began the building and planting for which he had been divinely commissioned.

SCHOOL OF THE PROPHETS

The Eastern Princess married Eochaidh, the Heremonn, upon a condition made by this notable patriarch that the Heremonn should abandon his former religion and build a college for the prophets. This he did, and the name of the school was Mur-Ollam, which is the name in both Hebrew and Irish for the school of the prophets.

YEAR OF JEREMIAH'S ARRIVAL

Mr. Thomas W. Plant in his article *The Date of Jeremiah's Arrival in Ireland,* DESTINY for March, 1938, refers to his visit at Glastonbury, in the summer of 1935 when the subject of Jeremiah's arrival in Ireland came up for discussion. He was asked by Mr. George Dansie of Bristol if he was interested in the decipherment of hieroglyphics. He was then shown a jumble of lines, circles, dots and spirals. Later, in a letter to Mr. Plant, Mr. Dansie wrote:

"These are the particulars that I gave you, when at Glastonbury, of the carved stone in the tomb of Ollam Fodhla, which is in Schiabhna-Cailliche, near Old Castle, Co. Meath, Ireland.

"It shows a Lunar Eclipse, in the constellation of Taurus, also a conjunction of the planets Saturn and Jupiter in Virgo.

"The prow of a ship is shown in the center, with five lines indicating the number of passengers it carries.

"On the left a part of the ship, which might be the stern, is shown and only four passengers, one having been left behind or lost as indicated by the line falling away from the ship. The wavy lines indicate the passage of the ship across the ocean, terminating at a central point on an island.

"Ollam Fodhla having been identified as Jeremiah, this stone would be a record of his journey from Egypt to Ireland, having in his care the two daughters of Zedekiah, and his scribe or secretary, Baruch, and probably an attendant for the two Princesses. [The

fifth passenger might have been Ebed-melech, the Ethiopian.]

"One of the Princesses appears to have been left at a country en route.

"The date of arrival according to the necessary stellar calculations made by an expert, V. E. Robson (a friend of Mr. Dansie), being *Thursday, 16th October, 583* B.C.

"At this date there was an eclipse of the moon in the constellation of Taurus, and a conjunction to within 10 degrees of Saturn and Jupiter in Virgo.

"The bird at the top may be a representation of Ezekiel's eagle which carried the tender twig to a mountain in Israel. (see Ezekiel 17: 1-7 & 22-24.)

"I believe the date of departure from Egypt was stated by Rev. W. M. H. Milner in an article or book, I cannot remember which, to be 584 B.C. At any rate, Mr. W. Campbell, writing in 1914, states that Jeremiah arrived in Ireland 230 years before the death of King Cimboath, which was in 353 B.C., and that, added to 230 years, gives us 583 B.C. See *Northern British-Israel Review*, Vol. 4, p. 171)."

EOCHAIDH, THE HEREMONN

Eochaidh, the Heremonn, changed the name of his capital city, Lothair, (sometimes spelled Cothair Croffin) to that of Tara. It is a well known fact that the Royal Arms of Ireland is the harp of David. Further, the crown which was worn by the sovereigns of that hitherto unaccounted for kingdom of Ireland had twelve points. Who shall say that "the King's daughter" was not planted there and that the first of the three of Ezekiel's overturns was not accomplished in the removal of the Royal line of David from Palestine to Ireland?

STONE OF DESTINY

Because their King had passed on before them to the unknown country into which Israel was later to be regathered, Hosea declares of them:

"For the children of Israel shall abide many days

without a king, and without a prince, and without a sacrifice, and without an image, and without an ephod, and without teraphim." (Hos. 3: 4.)

The marginal rendering of "without an image" is "without a standing pillar" while *Young's Analytical Concordance* gives other definitions, *i.e.*, "memorial stone, and pillar." Scholarly men who have investigated this passage in connection with its context give a correct rendering as "pillar rock and pillar stone."

Jeremiah journeyed from Egypt with this stone in his possession, and the other sacred emblems, and first landed in Spain from whence he sailed to Ireland according to the records. Beginning with Eochaidh, the Heremonn, and his young bride, Tea Tephi, who were crowned on this stone in Ireland, their descendants in succession were crowned on this stone of destiny.

The ancient kings of both the Danaan and Milesian races (being the same people) were for many ages crowned at Tara. This stone was sent to Scotland about 350 B.C. for the coronation of Fergus, King of Scots, who was a descendant of the Milesian Kings of Ireland. For many centuries this stone was used by the Scottish Kings in their coronation and was kept in the Abbey of Scone. This removal of the stone from Ireland to Scotland was its second overturn (Ezekiel 21: 27).

In 1297 A.D., when King Edward I invaded Scotland, the stone was taken to England and placed in Westminster Abbey where it has remained to this day. This removal from Scotland to England was the third and final overturn! Following this final overturn the promise is made that it will remain in its present resting place until He comes whose right it is.

There are many who object offhand, and without knowledge, that an assignment of a Luz-and-Jacob origin to the coronation stone is a matter of mere modern theory, the outgrowth of this school of literature since about 1837 A.D. But this is an untenable position, for it has been known as Jacob's stone ever since it reached Great Britain. The appelation, Jacob's stone, can be traced in the writings of William of Rislanger of Yorkshire who, writing in the 13th century (under A.D. 1292), records the coronation of King John Balliol "upon the stone on which Jacob placed his head."

In the *Encyclopedia Britannica* (Eleventh Edition) Vol. 14, page 569, under *Inisfail*, the following is stated:

"Inisfail, a poetical name for Ireland. It is derived from *Faul* or *Lia-fail*, the celebrated stone, identified in Irish legend with the stone on which the patriarch Jacob slept when he dreamed of the heavenly ladder. The Lia-fail was supposed to have been brought to Ireland by the Dedannans and set up at Tara as the 'inauguration stone' of the Irish kings; it was subsequently removed to Scone where it became the coronation stone of the Scottish kings, until it was taken by James VI, of Scotland to Westminster and placed under the coronation chair in the Abbey, where it has since remained. Inisfail was thus the island of the Fail, the island whose monarchs were crowned at Tara on the sacred inauguration stone."

The altars of ancient Ireland were called Botal, or Bothel, meaning House of God. That is, it is the Hebrew word *B-th-l* and has the same meaning. Hence, if this coronation stone which is in Westminster, which the English call Jacob's Pillow, and which their Scotch and Irish ancestors call "God's House" or "B-th-l," the "Stone of Destiny," is indeed what its names and history declare it to be, then it is the very throne of David upon which the sons of David were formerly crowned in the Temple of God at Jerusalem. This throne is now set over Israel regathered in the Isles. If all this is true, God has kept faith with David and preserved his throne through all generations as He promised.

EZEKIEL'S RIDDLE

While Jeremiah was lamenting in Jerusalem, Ezekiel, a fellow prophet of the school of the prophets, was among the captives by the river Chebar, far away in Chaldea, and to him the word of the Lord came, saying:

"Son of man, put forth a riddle and speak a parable unto the house of Israel." (Ez. 17: 1-2.)

Now a riddle is a hidden saying, something to be solved, while a parable is an allegory from which one is to draw a lesson. The fact that Ezekiel was to speak to the House of Israel and propound this riddle to them indicates that its solution lies with the House of Israel rather than with the House of Judah. We must, therefore, look to the House of Israel for the answer to the facts set forth in this riddle given by Ezekiel. The ten tribes had already been away from Palestine more than a hundred years and to them the prophet said:

"Thus saith the Lord God; A great eagle with great wings, long-winged, full of feathers, which had divers colours, came unto Lebanon, and took the highest branch of the cedar: He cropped off the top of his young twigs, and carried it into a land of traffick; he set it in a city of merchants." (Ez. 17: 3-4.)

PLANTING ZARAH'S LINE

Lebanon is a mountain range in Palestine and to this place the eagle—a means of transportation—came and removed a twig from the highest branch of a cedar of Lebanon. Now the cedar of Lebanon is symbolic of royalty. The twig from the seed of royalty is to be planted in a city of merchants, in a land of traffic, indicating the removal of a young royal personage from the land of Palestine to this place of planting. Ezekiel continues:

"He took also of the seed of the land, and planted it in a fruitful field; he placed it by great waters, and set it as a willow tree. And it grew, and became a spreading vine of low stature, whose branches turned toward him, and the roots thereof were under him: so it became a vine [Israel is His vine; see Jer. 2: 21], and brought forth branches, and shot forth sprigs." (Ez. 17: 5-6.)

ISRAEL TRANSPLANTED

The prophet is referring here to the lost tribes, their Assyrian captivity, their transplanting to a sea-girt sanctuary, to be followed by the advent of Tea Tephi, the tender twig, to the chief city in their distant land of commerce. The location is given as by *great waters*. This was not the Mediterranean or Great Sea of Scripture but evidently referred to the great ocean, or the Atlantic Ocean, as we know this body of water today. Here was the new home of the House of Israel where this seed of Israel (not Judah) was planted. Ezekiel continues:

"There was also another great eagle with great wings and many feathers: and behold, this vine did bend her roots toward him, and shot forth her branches toward him, that he might water it by the furrows of her plantation. It was planted in a good soil by great waters, that it might bring forth branches, and that it might bear fruit, that it might be a goodly vine." (Ez. 17: 7-8.)

ARRIVAL OF TEA TEPHI

Here is a record of the arrival of another personage to the good soil by great waters, brought there by the same means of transportation used to bring the sons of Zarah. This is not the same eagle, but "another" eagle, or ship, the embroidered wings [marginal rendering of "divers colored wings"] were its sails. This was no doubt a ship of Dan since "Dan abode in ships." This tribe took cedars of Lebanon to make masts for their ships and we also know that the seaport of Tyre in Palestine was the port into which they came for these cedars.

Rev. J. H. Allen, in his book *Judah's Sceptre and Joseph's Birthright,** says:

"We are forced to the conclusion that the object which the writer has in view in mentioning the coming of the second ship is, that we may guess that another important personage has arrived; for, after mentioning the ship's arrival, his next expression is: 'Behold this vine did bend her roots toward him.'

"Then, still under the similitude of a vine, and that which is essential to its life and growth, *viz.,* land and water, there follows that which clearly indicates a unity of life, claims and purposes. In fact, there was a marriage between the *her* and the *him* of this riddle, the result of which she, too, was *set* or *planted* in that land of a *goodly vine,* albeit that goodly vine is of *low stature,* and bore fruit, that is, offspring."

But a prince must wed a princess and Jeremiah's mission to build and to plant had to do with the royal charges under his care, one of whom was to marry in the appointed place a prince of the line of Judah through Zarah, who also had been carried to that land by a great eagle or ship.

JUDGMENT UPON THE PHAREZ LINE

"Shall it prosper? shall he not pull up the roots thereof, and cut off the fruit thereof, that it wither? it shall wither in all the leaves of her spring, even without great power or many people to pluck it up by the roots thereof. Yea, behold, being planted, shall it pros-

*$3.00 postpaid. Destiny Publishers, Merrimac, Mass. 01860

per? shall it not utterly wither, when the east wind
toucheth it? it shall wither in the furrows where it
grew." (Ez. 17: 9-10.)

With the birth of a son to the young royal couple,
an heir to the throne was born of the line of Zarah
through his father. Thus, though Tea Tephi of the line
of Pharez was "planted" and "prospered" as the beloved wife of Eochaidh, yet, because the reigning line
continued through a son of Zarah's line, the phrase of
the riddle was also fulfilled in her which states, "it
shall wither [i.e., the Pharez line] in the furrows
[isles] where it grew."

This same message is also addressed to the rebellious
house of Zedekiah and the next eleven verses (11-21)
identify this part of the riddle by deliberately explain-
ing it.

Having pronounced doom upon Judah and Zedekiah
the prophet returns to the theme of Israel and the royal,
or tender, twig to be planted in the mountain of the
height of Israel:

"I will also take of the highest branch of the high
cedar, and will set it; I will crop off from the top of his
young twigs a tender one, and will plant it upon an high
mountain and eminent: In the mountain of the height
of Israel will I plant it; and it shall bring forth boughs,
and bear fruit, and be a goodly cedar: and under it shall
dwell all fowl of every wing; in the shadow of the
branches thereof shall they dwell. And all the trees of
the field shall know that I the Lord have brought down
the high tree, have exalted the low tree, have dried up

the green tree, and have made the dry tree to flourish:
I the Lord have spoken and have done it." (Ez. 17:
22-24.)

God had removed the crown from the head of Zedekiah of the line of Pharez and placed it upon the head
of a prince of the line of Zarah, who was united in marriage with Tea Tephi, the daughter of Zedekiah and
heiress to David's Throne, when, as Jeremiah's ward,
she was brought in a sailing vessel to the Emerald Isle.
Thus, the high tree, Judah in Palestine, was brought
down and the low tree, Israel cast away and in captivity,
was exalted, and the green tree, the House of Pharez,
was dried up and the dry tree, the House of Zarah,
flourished.

We leave Jeremiah in the Isles, who commenced his
mission to build and to plant under very auspicious conditions, far removed from the turmoil and strife which
had afflicted him in the lands of Palestine and Egypt.

APPENDIX

WHICH GENEALOGY?

The importance of establishing the genealogy of Jesus Christ through Mary, His mother, is of more than academic interest. It is essential that it be established for only thus can the legality of the claims made for Jesus Christ be confirmed, for they rest upon the verification of Mary's descent from the House of David, and that she is the virgin of whom Isaiah prophesied. (Isa. 7: 14.) Modern scholarship, whose findings are generally followed by the theologian today, has selected the genealogy given by Luke to be that of Mary and that given by Matthew has been assigned to Joseph, the husband of Mary.

We appreciate that raising this genealogical issue will cause controversy, but rather than simply accept the findings of even the scholars without adequate proof, it is well to re-examine all the evidence presented by both witnesses, Matthew and Luke. To the evidence they furnish let us add the testimony of others and bring the apparent divergent views into the light, examining the text and context to see if there is a sane and logical solution to the seeming discrepancy between the two genealogical tables. It is admitted by all that there is a problem to be dealt with, no matter which genealogical table is selected as that of Mary, the mother of our Lord.

For the sake of expediency, let us assume both sides have given their testimony and each has rested his case.

The judge sums up the evidence. He would proceed something like this:

Matthew, on the witness stand under direct examination, has testified that he is endeavoring to show that Mary, the mother of Jesus, is of the line of David in fulfillment of the promise to the House of David that a virgin would conceive and bear a son. He gave the complete genealogy of the mother of Jesus Christ, then the account of the birth of her son, and his exact words as he finished his testimony were:

"Now all this was done, that it might be fulfilled which was spoken of the Lord by the prophet [Isaiah], saying, Behold, a virgin shall be with child, and shall bring forth a son, and they shall call his name Emmanuel, which being interpreted is, God with us." (Matt. 1: 22-23.)

When questioned as to whose genealogy he was recording, Matthew stated it was "the book of the generations of Jesus Christ, the son of David" (Matt. 1: 1). Thus, at the very beginning of his testimony Matthew declares he is giving the genealogy of Jesus Christ. It is very evident from the record itself that Matthew intended to give the genealogical line of Mary if, as he has said, he was giving the genealogy of Jesus Christ, the son of Mary. He could not be giving the genealogy of Joseph, the husband of Mary, if he intended to give the genealogy of Jesus Christ, for he states that Jesus was born of a virgin.

But Matthew's record gives Joseph as the husband of Mary. When questioned further, Matthew shows a check in his account which should place everyone on guard against an apparent error in his testimony. The check was in numbering the genealogical line of Jesus Christ by dividing it into three groups of fourteen generations each as follows:

"So all the generations from Abraham to David are fourteen generations; and from David until the carrying away into Babylon are fourteen generations; and from the carrying away into Babylon unto Christ are fourteen generations." (Matt. 1: 17.)

Matthew's tabulation clearly shows that the first two groups as given contain fourteen generations each, but the final group contains only thirteen generations if the Joseph of his genealogy is the husband of Mary. However, if this Joseph is the *father* of Mary, there are fourteen generations. It would seem that a copyist has made an error in recording Matthew's tabulation, for Luke declares the father of Joseph, the husband of Mary, is Heli, while the father of the Joseph listed by Matthew is Jacob. These two Josephs cannot be the same person.

Summing up the testimony given by Matthew, it is clear that he was primarily interested in proving that Mary is the virgin of the line of David who would bring forth a son in accordance with Isaiah's prophecy. This is in harmony with his opening statement when he said that his purpose was to give the genealogy of Jesus Christ and, if this is so, it conforms with the required three sets given of fourteen generations each—if the Joseph of Matthew's genealogical table is the father and not the husband of Mary. We must assume that Matthew placed these checks in his record for the purpose of enabling the rectification of just such an error as appears when Joseph, the son of Jacob, is called the husband of Mary instead of her father. If one insists that the Joseph to whom Matthew refers is the husband of Mary, then it is necessary to explain the error which gives only thirteen generations from the captivity to Christ, whereas there should be fourteen according to Matthew's statement. In addition to this, one would have to declare that Matthew was in error in trying to prove Mary is the virgin of prophecy. Not only would it be pointless for Matthew to refer to Mary as the virgin of David's line if he was not dealing with her genealogy, but to give the genealogical line of her husband would contradict the position he proposed to maintain—that Christ was born of a virgin—and jeopardize his testimony regarding Mary, which would be without foundation in fact. The failure to rectify *one* error, therefore, by changing the word *husband* to *father*, produces at least three major errors to take its place.

Now let us turn to Luke's testimony (Luke 3:23 -38). We find, first, his definite declaration that he was giving the genealogy of Joseph, *the supposed father* of Jesus. At no time does he mention the name of Mary in connection with this genealogical record. It is safe to assume he does not mention her name because he was not dealing with her ancestors, but with those of her husband. He testified that Jesus was the supposed son of Joseph, who was of Heli, who was of Matthat. The translators have added *the son* to make it read *the son of* and modern scholars have made this mean *son-in-law* to justify their selection of the genealogy of Joseph given in Luke's Gospel as the genealogy of Mary.

Comparing the testimony given by Matthew with that of Luke, it is reasonable to assume that one of the Josephs named must be the father of Mary and the other her husband, for Matthew declares Joseph's father was Jacob, while Luke states the father of the Joseph he was dealing with was Heli. These two Josephs cannot be the same individual and so, since we must harmonize the three sets of fourteen generations given in Matthew's testimony, this can only be done by making Joseph, the son of Jacob, the father of Mary, since Joseph, of Heli, is her husband. This conclusion strengthens the text and not only brings Matthew's and Luke's testimonies into harmony but the genealogical tables of each become meaningful. Matthew is giving that of the mother of Jesus, proving that Mary is the virgin of the line of David, while Luke mentions that of Joseph, the supposed father of Jesus.

If we fail to rectify what appears to have been a copyist's error, and which is definitely out of harmony with the genealogical check of the fourteen generations given by the Holy Spirit through Matthew, it replaces one error with five major errors. Three of these are in Matthew's Gospel and two are in Luke's. Matthew's testimony is that he is dealing with (*1*) the genealogy of Jesus and (*2*) is proving that Mary is the virgin of the line of David, which must be rejected if his genealogical table is assigned to Joseph, (*3*) the husband of

Mary. If Luke's testimony that he is dealing with the genealogy of (4) the supposed father of Jesus is rejected, (5) adding words which do not appear in the text, the context must be changed to make it apply to Mary whom he does not even mention. Surely the scholars bring about increased confusion in the results of their deliberations and their approach to this subject emphasizes our Lord's appraisal of blind leaders whom He said, "Strain at a gnat, and swallow a camel" (Matt. 23: 24).

— H. B. R.

INDEX OF SCRIPTURAL TEXTS

CONCORDANCE

Yoke — *Cont.*
  Neck of Israel, 172
Yokes
  Made by Jeremiah, 153

Zarah
  Ambitions of, 286
  Branch of Judah's posterity, 285
  Line of, 288
  Prince of, 299
  The dry tree, 299
Zarah's Line
  Planted, 295
Zebudah, 115
Zechariah, 12
Zedekiah, 190, 249
  Advised, 155
  Advised to surrender, 233
  Basket of bad figs, 141
  Birth of, 117

Zedekiah — *Cont.*
  Calls a conference, 152
  Daughter of, 288, 299
  Daughters of, 243, 279
  Deliver into hand of Nebuchadnezzar, 111
  Failed the test, 216
  Inheritance passed, 204
  King of Judah, 109, 121
  Mother of, 276
  Powerless, 232
  Prophecy concerning, 211
  Rebellious house of, 298
  Removed crown from, 299
  Sons slain, 128
  The prophet, 165
  Threw off allegiance, 227
  To Babylon, 274
  Told his prophets lied, 156
  Took flight, 234

Zedekiah — *Cont.*
  Warns, 226
Zelophehad
  Daughters of, 204, 280
Zephaniah, 12, 165
Zidon, 153, 260
Zimri, 285
Zion
  Bring you to, 31
  Escape from, 282
  Evil done in, 271
  Law shall go forth, 201
  Put on thy strength, 29
  Restored, 175
  Shall be plowed, 149
  Way of, 265
Zionists, 107
Zodiac
  Not to heed, 57
  Sign of Virgo, 130